EXERCISE BOOK
to accompany

Rosen

THE ACADEMIC WRITER'S HANDBOOK

Kathryn Riley
University of Minnesota Duluth

PEARSON
Longman

New York Boston San Francisco
London Toronto Sydney Tokyo Singapore Madrid
Mexico City Munich Paris Cape Town Hong Kong Montreal

Exercise Book to accompany Rosen, *The Academic Writer's Handbook*

Copyright ©2006 Pearson Education, Inc.

All rights reserved. Printed in the United States of America. Instructors may reproduce portions of this book for classroom use only. All other reproductions are strictly prohibited without prior permission of the publisher, except in the case of brief quotations embodied in critical articles and reviews.

ISBN: 0-321-36283-7

3 4 5 6 7 8 9 10–CW–08 07

CONTENTS

Note: The corresponding chapter in *The Academic Writer's Handbook* is indicated in parentheses.

Chapter 1	Constructing Sentences (Chapter 28)	1
Chapter 2	Correcting Sentence Fragments (Chapter 29)	11
Chapter 3	Correcting Comma Splices and Fused Sentences (Chapter 30)	19
Chapter 4	Using Verbs (Chapter 31)	29
Chapter 5	Correcting Errors in Subject-Verb Agreement (Chapter 32)	41
Chapter 6	Using Adjectives and Adverbs (Chapter 33)	47
Chapter 7	Correcting Misplaced and Dangling Modifiers (Chapter 34)	53
Chapter 8	Using Nouns and Pronouns (Chapter 35)	61
Chapter 9	Correcting Errors in Pronoun-Antecedent Agreement and Reference (Chapter 36)	67
Chapter 10	Correcting Errors in Consistency (Chapter 37)	77
Chapter 11	Correcting Faulty Parallelism (Chapter 38)	87
Chapter 12	Being Clear, Concise, and Direct (Chapter 39)	97
Chapter 13	Building Emphasis with Coordination and Subordination (Chapter 40)	109
Chapter 14	Choosing the Right Word (Chapter 41)	121
Chapter 15	Using End Punctuation (Chapter 42)	137
Chapter 16	Using Commas (Chapter 43)	143
Chapter 17	Using Semicolons (Chapter 44)	155
Chapter 18	Using Apostrophes (Chapter 45)	163
Chapter 19	Using Quotation Marks (Chapter 46)	171
Chapter 20	Using Other Marks (Chapter 47)	179
Chapter 21	Using Capitals (Chapter 48)	187
Chapter 22	Using Italics (Chapter 49)	193
Chapter 23	Using Abbreviations (Chapter 50)	197
Chapter 24	Using Numbers (Chapter 51)	203
Chapter 25	Using Hyphens (Chapter 52)	207
Chapter 26	Making Spelling Decisions (Chapter 53)	213

ANSWERS TO SELECTED EXERCISES

Chapter 1	Constructing Sentences	221
Chapter 2	Correcting Sentence Fragments	222
Chapter 3	Correcting Comma Splices and Fused Sentences	223
Chapter 4	Using Verbs	225
Chapter 5	Correcting Errors in Subject-Verb Agreement	226
Chapter 6	Using Adjectives and Adverbs	227
Chapter 7	Correcting Misplaced and Dangling Modifiers	228
Chapter 8	Using Nouns and Pronouns	229
Chapter 9	Correcting Errors in Pronoun-Antecedent Agreement and Reference	231
Chapter 10	Correcting Errors in Consistency	232
Chapter 11	Correcting Faulty Parallelism	234
Chapter 12	Being Clear, Concise, and Direct	235
Chapter 13	Building Emphasis with Coordination and Subordination	237
Chapter 14	Choosing the Right Word	239
Chapter 15	Using End Punctuation	242
Chapter 16	Using Commas	243
Chapter 17	Using Semicolons	246
Chapter 18	Using Apostrophes	247
Chapter 19	Using Quotation Marks	249
Chapter 20	Using Other Marks	250
Chapter 21	Using Capitals	251
Chapter 22	Using Italics	252
Chapter 23	Using Abbreviations	253
Chapter 24	Using Numbers	253
Chapter 25	Using Hyphens	254
Chapter 26	Making Spelling Decisions	255

PREFACE

This exercise book is designed to accompany *The Academic Writer's Handbook*. It contains exercises keyed to Chapters 28 through 53 of the handbook.

Content for exercises is drawn from various disciplines; exercises include both discrete sentences and connected discourse, depending on the nature of the material under discussion. Appropriate chapters end with review exercises designed to allow students to practice individual skills mastered within the chapter. Some review exercises refer students to textbooks in other courses, reinforcing the interdisciplinary theme of the handbook, while others call for students to work with their own writing.

Answers to selected exercises are found at the back of this book. A full set of answers is available to instructors in a separate answer key.

CHAPTER 1

Constructing Sentences

For use with Chapter 28 of *The Academic Writer's Handbook*

EXERCISE 1-1: Implicit understanding of sentences

This exercise is designed to show you just how much you really do know about sentences. In the following paragraph, mark off with a slash (/) places where you'd end a sentence. (You can also supply commas where you think they're needed, but that's not necessary for the purposes of this exercise.) Then compare your response to other students' responses. As you discuss differences, try to explain why you divided the paragraph as you did. (There are several different ways of dividing the paragraph.)

The Supreme Court hears about 125 to 130 cases during the seven months each year that it is in session these cases are chosen from over 5,000 petitions most of which are prepared by highly specialized law firms but every year 200 to 300 petitions are submitted by individuals on their own behalf these cases are called *pro se* the Latin words for "for himself" in most years no more than one or two *pro se* cases are heard and fewer result in a positive decision many of these petitions are prepared by prisoners who have given up on lawyers one of the most famous cases was that of Clarence Gideon a poor man who was convicted without having been represented by a lawyer Gideon's petition which he wrote out by hand was accepted by the Court and resulted in a landmark ruling that people who can't afford lawyers must be given the opportunity to be represented by a court-appointed lawyer.

EXERCISE 1-2: Recognizing subjects and predicates

In the following sentences, place a slash (/) between subjects and predicates. Then underline the simple subject once, and the simple predicate twice.

EXAMPLE: <u>Nations</u> embarking on military adventures / often <u><u>invoke</u></u> a deity to justify their cause.

1. The Roman emperor Titus ceremoniously called upon the Roman god of war, Mars, when he attacked Jerusalem in A.D. 70.

2. The prophet Muhammad, founder of Islam, attributed his A.D. 630 conquest of Mecca to the power of Allah.

3. Allah, the one true god of Islam, apparently was also responsible for the victory over Jerusalem in 1187.

4. The sacking of Constantinople during the Fourth Crusade in 1204 was undertaken in the name of the Christian god.

5. The historical term "Crusades" refers to the Christian invasions of the Holy Land, which was then under the control of Muslims.

6. The Muslims themselves had a term for Holy Wars, "jihad."

7. The revolt of the Shi'ite Muslims in 685 pitted against each other two forces, both claiming the protection of Allah.

8. Union and Confederate forces in the American Civil War both claimed to be fighting for the same Christian god almost eighteen centuries later.

9. The Japanese forces that bombed Pearl Harbor in 1941 were fighting for the Emperor, who was considered the "son of heaven."

10. The Gulf War of 1990-91 between Iraq and a U.S.-led coalition again saw two armies each invoking the name of a god.

EXERCISE 1-3: Recognizing subjects, predicates, and parts of speech

Make a photocopy of a brief passage from a textbook in one of your other courses. In order to practice identifying sentence parts and parts of speech, mark off the simple subjects and simple predicates according to the instructions for Exercise 1-2, and then, using abbreviations ("n"-noun, "v"-verb, "adj"-adjective, "adv"-adverb, "pro"-pronoun, "prep"-preposition, "con"-conjunction, and—if there are any—"int"-interjection), try to identify as many parts of speech as you can.

EXERCISE 1-4: Understanding basic sentence patterns

For each of the following sentences, place a slash (/) between the subject and predicate, and then identify with the appropriate abbreviation each of the following: *v*—verb, *v (tr)*—transitive verb, *v (l)*—linking verb, *do*—direct object, *io*—indirect object, *oc*—object complement, and *sc*—subject complement. Finally, on the lines at the right, identify by number the basic sentence pattern.

$$\qquad\qquad\qquad v(tr) \quad\ do$$
EXAMPLE: Architects / design buildings

1. Friedrich Kekule was an architecture student. _____

2. Kekule found chemistry preferable. _____

3. His chemistry career flourished. _____

4. Organic chemistry became Kekule's specialty. _____

5. Kekule gave organic chemistry a structural theory. _____

EXERCISE 1-5: Using single-word modifiers

For each of the following sentences, underline the nouns once and the verbs twice. Then rewrite the sentences, using one-word adjectives or adverbs to modify the nouns and verbs.

EXAMPLE: Rock <u>musicians</u> <u>make</u> concert <u>appearances</u>.

REVISION: Popular rock musicians frequently make lucrative concert appearances.

1. Fans scream.
2. Promoters make money.
3. Musicians become exhausted.
4. An album can make a musician famous
5. A musician needs music videos.

EXERCISE 1-6: Recognizing phrases

Identify the type of phrase underlined and its function in the sentence.

preposition/adj.
EXAMPLE: Nuclear energy, <u>with all its problems</u>, seems to be here to stay.

1. People have a right <u>to know how dangerous it is</u>.
2. The industry, <u>feeling besieged</u>, is engaging in a public relations campaign.

3. Nuclear power is the cleaner <u>of the two primary power sources</u>, nuclear and fossil fuel.

4. <u>Until appropriate waste-removal methods are devised</u>, nuclear remains the most dangerous power source.

5. <u>Generating wind and solar power</u> is a dream of some researchers.

6. Many people would refuse <u>to pay the costs involved with solar power</u>.

7. <u>Their lives shortened by lung disease</u>, many coal miners attest to the dangers of that fuel.

8. Experts are abandoning research into oil, <u>convinced of its political dependence</u>.

9. Researchers are constantly trying <u>to solve energy problems</u>.

10. Nobody knows what will be <u>the energy source of the future</u>.

EXERCISE 1-7: Modifying sentences with phrases

Take the following basic sentences and add modifiers and modifiers within modifiers, making sure to keep the sentence coherent. (The point at which one more modifier would make the sentence "topple" is the point at which to stop adding.) Compare your responses to those of other students: Do your responses differ primarily in style? meaning? both?

1. Arturo sang.

2. Keisha taught Mary Ellen the dance.

3. The members welcomed the nonmembers.

4. Ben, Alicia, and Samantha were the stars.

5. The performers made their parents proud.

EXERCISE 1-8: Modifying sentences with dependent clauses

Combine the following pairs of sentences, using subordinate conjunctions and relative pronouns to create dependent clauses.

EXAMPLE: American artist Ad Reinhardt was the son of immigrants. He became famous for his single-color paintings.

REVISION: American artist Ad Reinhardt, *who was the son of immigrants*, became famous for his single-color paintings.

1. Reinhardt was an abstract painter from the beginning of his career. Other painters embraced abstractionism at some point in their careers.

2. Picasso said, "My painting represents the victory of the forces of light and peace over the powers of darkness and evil." Reinhardt responded with, "My painting represents the victory of the forces of darkness and peace over the powers of light and evil."

3. Picasso represented reverence and ideology. Reinhardt represented irreverence and iconoclasm.

4. Reinhardt's "black" paintings seem so filled with nothingness. The viewer must stand and stare for a long time.

5. Art lovers flocked to the Los Angeles Museum of Contemporary Art in October, 1991. An Ad Reinhardt retrospective was being exhibited.

EXERCISE 1-9: Identifying sentence structures

Identify the following sentences as simple, compound, complex, or compound-complex.

EXAMPLE: Legends of everyday horrors last for generations. (simple)

1. Although many people tell the tale of the psychopath's hook left dangling on the car door handle, nobody has ever produced any evidence that it really happened.

2. Probably because of its pathos, the story of the dog tied to the car bumper still survives, and it was immortalized in the movie *National Lampoon's Vacation*.

3. The notice of the LSD-laced children's stamps has made the round for years, but nobody has ever seen one.

4. A famous academic story involves the philosophy examination question, "Why?" and the student's response, "Why not?"

5. This story and its variations all report that the professor, appreciating creativity, gave the student an A.

EXERCISE 1-10: Review

Rewrite the following paragraph, combining sentences by converting some into single-word modifiers, phrases, and dependent clauses. You may also combine sentences by joining independent clauses with conjunctions.

Personal ownership is a concept. The concept is not innate in human nature. Native Americans did not own land. They had an idea. They belonged to the land. They could use the land. They drew their livelihood from the land. The notion of ownership was peculiar to them. The notion was from the west. The peculiarity can be seen. Consider ownership of air. Consider ownership of the seas. Ownership is personal. This is a notion. The notion seems absurd. We think about the notion of personal ownership. We begin to wonder. We wonder about its legitimacy.

CHAPTER 2

Correcting Sentence Fragments

For use with Chapter 29 of *The Academic Writer's Handbook*

EXERCISE 2-1: Identifying fragments

Using the three-part test, identify and explain the fragments in the sentences below. Circle the number of any complete sentences.

EXAMPLE: Beginning in Anaheim, California in 1955.

ANALYSIS: Fragment—no verb.

1. Hailed as the prototype amusement park of the 20th century.

2. Because Disneyland California had been so wildly successful.

3. With the 1971 opening of Walt Disney World in Orlando, Florida.

4. And soon became one of the most popular tourist attractions in the country.

5. But Disney Enterprises wasn't content with the success of Disneyland and Disney World.

6. A new park that provided a glimpse of the future.

7. A place called Experimental Prototype Community of Tomorrow, or EPCOT.

8. Followed by the 1983 opening of Tokyo Disneyland.

9. Despite protests by French citizens concerned about the effect of the new Euro Disneyland outside Paris.

10. However, Euro Disneyland has been tremendously successful.

EXERCISE 2-2: Identifying and correcting dependent clause fragments

The paragraph below contains five fragments formed by setting off dependent clauses as complete sentences. Correct each of the fragments by joining the dependent clauses to independent clauses.

EXAMPLE: Sociologists study how humans behave. When they are in groups.

REVISION: Sociologists study how humans behave when they are in groups.

Social communities have been recognized among humans for thousands of years. But it is only within the last century. That humans have become aware of social communities among other animals. After studying primates, and monkeys in particular. Researchers have concluded that these creatures have relatively sophisticated methods of communication, employing different sounds to signal different meanings. Because calls warning of danger are recognizably different from calls indicating the approach of another monkey. Researchers believe that their "language" is based on survival skills. There is also a hierarchy among members of monkey groups, especially among vervet monkeys. Vervets identify themselves according to family, community, and social rank, and their behavior is governed by some concept of social relationships. In this way, vervets are very much like humans. Who also define themselves in terms of their relationships to others. Although vervets do not have the intellectual capacity of humans. Their communities often run far more smoothly than those of their human counterparts.

EXERCISE 2-3: Identifying and correcting phrase fragments

In the pairs of sentences below, identify each fragment by naming the type of phrase it represents and correct the fragments by joining phrases to independent clauses. Circle the number of any sentence that is correct.

EXAMPLE: <u>To collect great art</u>. One must have a good deal of money. (infinitive phrase)

REVISION: <u>To collect great art</u>, one must have a good deal of money.

1. Walter H. Annenberg is a great art collector. Having spent a considerable fortune on works by the world's most renowned painters.

2. The son of an immigrant who ended up in jail for tax evasion. Annenberg overcame many obstacles in his own rise to success.

3. Throughout his life, Annenberg has been known for his philanthropy. Particularly making substantial donations to many art museums.

4. One of Annenberg's prize possessions is his Impressionist collection. One of the finest collections in the world.

Correcting Sentence Fragments   15

5. This collection, as well as Annenberg's Post-Impressionist collection, will go to New York's Metropolitan Museum of Art. After his death.

6. In 1991. The Annenberg collection toured the country.

7. Among the collection's stops were museums in New York, Philadelphia, Los Angeles, and Washington, D.C.

8. Museums hosting the tour have been rewarded with increased attendance. Providing them with much-needed additional funds.

9. The collection includes paintings by Renoir, Gauguin, and Monet. Three of the most highly respected Impressionists of their day.

10. The Metropolitan Museum is fortunate indeed. To know that the collection will one day hang on its walls.

EXERCISE 2-4: Identifying and correcting fragments caused by repeating and compound elements

In the pairs of sentences below, identify the fragments formed by repeating elements and compound predicates and join them to the independent clauses. Circle the number of any sentence that is correct.

EXAMPLE: The international community is becoming more aware of how nations deal with crime and punishment. Especially punishment.

REVISION: The international community is becoming more aware of how nations deal with crime and punishment—especially punishment.

1. The United States is one of a decreasing number of prominent nations to use capital punishment. Otherwise known as the death penalty.

2. In extradition cases, the United States currently faces a problem. A serious problem.

3. Countries that have outlawed capital punishment question the U.S. policy. And sometimes refuse to extradite suspects facing the death penalty here.

4. Countries that still use capital punishment include China, South Africa, and Cuba. And, of course, the United States.

5. The extradition problem is extremely sensitive. So sensitive that leaders are often reluctant to discuss it.

EXERCISE 2-5: Review

In the following paragraph, correct fragments either by creating independent clauses or by joining the fragments to independent clauses. Underline any fragment that seems particularly effective.

Martha Graham was one of the most prominent names in dance in the 20th century. Rejecting traditional ballet. Graham brought dancers to the floor first. There they contracted their bodies. And felt the pull of gravity. In her early Vaudeville days she played more than one fighting woman. This image recurred throughout her career. Which spanned six decades. Graham's style was known for its intensity and fierceness as well as for its beauty. Although she rejected tradition. She eventually began a tradition of her own. It is a considerable understatement. To say that Graham influenced virtually every choreographer in modern dance. However, her influence extended beyond dance itself to theater and film. Among her students were many well-known figures. Great actresses such as Bette Davis. Davis considered Graham a genius.

Who had revolutionized the world of dance and movement. Graham was 96 years old when she died, but her legacy will live on. Forever.

CHAPTER 3

Correcting Comma Splices and Fused Sentences

For use with Chapter 30 of *The Academic Writer's Handbook*

EXERCISE 3-1: Identifying fused sentences and comma splices

Identify each of the following sentences as a fused sentence (*f*) or comma splice (*cs*). Then use a slash (/) to indicate the point at which the sentence should be separated.

EXAMPLE: The medicine chest is an important part of any home, you don't need to spend a lot of money to keep it well-stocked.

REVISION: The medicine chest is an important part of any home, / you don't need to spend a lot of money to keep it well-stocked.

1. One of the most basic items in the medicine chest isn't normally considered a medicine at all it's usually found in the kitchen cabinets.

2. Baking soda can be used a number of ways, it can be a deodorant, a salve for mosquito bites or poison ivy, a toothpaste or mouthwash, or an antacid.

3. Tea can also be used to soothe bites or sunburn it should not be used on a serious burn.
4. Another kitchen staple that can do double duty is vinegar, mixed with water it can be used to relieve "swimmer's ear."
5. Many of today's adults recall drinking ginger ale to soothe an upset stomach, carbonated drinks of any kind still do the trick.
6. Among first-aid items that should be in a medicine chest are Band-Aids, cotton balls, and tweezers, rubbing alcohol is important, too.
7. The well-stocked medicine chest should also have medicines aspirin or nonaspirin pain reliever, decongestant, and cough syrup are medicine-chest staples.
8. The medicine chest is no place for children, precautions should be taken in homes with small children.
9. Some people have overstocked medicine chests others don't have even the bare necessities.
10. Every home should have basic supplies what's in the medicine chest depends on the needs of the family.

EXERCISE 3-2: Revising comma splices and fused sentences

Rewrite each of the following sentences from Exercise 3-1 as specified in parentheses.

EXAMPLE: The medicine chest is an important part of any home, you don't need to spend a lot of money to keep it well-stocked. (coordinate conjunction)

REVISION: The medicine chest is an important part of any home, *and* you don't need to spend a lot of money to keep it well-stocked.

1. One of the most basic items in the medicine chest isn't normally considered a medicine at all it's usually found in the kitchen cabinets. (semicolon & conjunctive adverb)

2. Baking soda can be used a number of ways, it can be a deodorant, a salve for mosquito bites or poison ivy, a toothpaste or mouthwash, or an antacid. (colon)

3. Tea can also be used to soothe bites or sunburn it should not be used on a serious burn. (period & conjunctive adverb)

4. Another kitchen staple that can do double duty is vinegar, mixed with water it can be used to relieve "swimmer's ear." (colon)

5. Many of today's adults recall drinking ginger ale to soothe an upset stomach, carbonated drinks of any kind still do the trick. (semicolon)

6. Among first-aid items that should be in a medicine chest are band aids, cotton balls, and tweezers, rubbing alcohol is important, too. (period & conjunctive adverb)

7. The well-stocked medicine chest should also have medicines aspirin or nonaspirin pain reliever, decongestant, and cough syrup are medicine-chest staples. (semicolon & transitional expression)

8. The medicine chest is no place for children, precautions should be taken in homes with small children. (semicolon & conjunctive adverb)

9. Some people have overstocked medicine chests others don't have even the bare necessities. (comma & subordinating conjunction)

10. Every home should have basic supplies what's in the medicine chest depends on the needs of the family. (comma & subordinating conjunction)

EXERCISE 3-3: Revising comma splices and fused sentences

Correct each of the following comma splices and fused sentences in two different ways. Be prepared to discuss the effect of punctuating the sentences differently.

EXAMPLE: Humans have been fascinated by time travel at least since the days of H. G. Wells, Einstein's theories took the notion out of the realm of science fiction.

REVISION 1: Humans have been fascinated by time travel at least since the days of H. G. Wells; however, Einstein's theories took the notion out of the realm of science fiction.

REVISION 2: Although humans have been fascinated by time travel at least since the days of H. G. Wells, Einstein's theories took the notion out of the realm of science fiction.

1. One of Wells's most famous novels was *The Time Machine* it introduced Victorian society to the fascination of time travel.

2. Einstein declared time to be the fourth dimension, suddenly physicists began to think of traveling in time as they thought of traveling through space.

3. The laws of physics don't include anything to indicate that time travel is impossible the possibility calls into question the foundations of physics.

4. On the one hand, time travel should be theoretically possible, on the other, the implications of time travel upset the laws of physics.

5. In general terms, the implications involve laws of cause and effect how can the effect come before the cause, which is what time travel would allow?

6. More specific questions abound, what would happen if a person traveled back in time and somehow killed her grandmother?

7. A physicist from Princeton University, J. Richard Gott, has constructed a theoretical time machine its journey would involve movement around a pair of "cosmic strings."

8. At the California Institute of Technology, a similar machine was designed it would speed through a "wormhole."

9. Laypersons have difficulty understanding the complex theories behind these models they do have access to more fanciful time machines.

10. When they think about traveling through time, most people would prefer a more glamorous machine Doc's Delorean in *Back to the Future* fits the bill perfectly.

EXERCISE 3-4: Review

Rewrite the following paragraph, correcting the comma splices and fused sentences by using different strategies. As you determine which strategies to use, keep in mind the smooth flow of sentences as well as the correctness of the sentences.

In some totalitarian countries, citizens worry about the governments listening in on their private conversations, monitoring their movements, and generally invading their privacy. Most United States citizens rarely worry about such government intrusion, a very real threat to privacy does exist. That threat comes from business. Certainly the FBI and state or local police organizations collect information on certain citizens the DMI has information on thousands. The DMI, or Direct Marketing Information, sells mailing lists to businesses that use the mails to contact potential customers, many of these businesses can also get information on individuals' buying habits, their family size, their income and savings records, and many other areas that most of us consider quite private. This invasion of privacy is a result primarily of the technology boom the existence of cordless phones, the sophistication of computers, and the emergence of voicemail systems on telephone networks all contribute to the problem. The invasion-of-privacy business is also aided by the government. It's not that the government regularly sells information on private citizens, it's that the government does little to prevent others from doing so. Regulations on business steadily declined throughout the 1980s now it seems to be open season on citizens' private lives.

EXERCISE 3-5: Revising

Look through your graded papers to find instructors' comments regarding fragments, fused sentences, and/or comma splices. Reread the papers, identifying the errors as you read by using the guidelines presented in the text. Then revise the errors. (If you don't have any graded papers handy, look through any body of writing you've done recently.)

CHAPTER 4

Using Verbs

For use with Chapter 31 of *The Academic Writer's Handbook*

EXERCISE 4-1: Using irregular verbs

Choose five of the irregular verbs (other than *be*) from the list provided in the text. For each verb, construct three sentences: one using the base form, one using the past tense form, and one using the past participle form. (If you have difficulty using the past participle form, consult the sections on tense and voice.)

EXAMPLE: The bells *ring* every hour.
　　　　　　 The bells *rang* all through the night.
　　　　　　 The bells *have rung* at noon for fifty years.

Verb 1

Verb 2

Verb 3

Verb 4

Verb 5

EXERCISE 4-2: Identifying main and auxiliary verbs

Underline and identify the main verb and any auxiliary verbs associated with it in the following sentences. (Remember that the verbs *be* and *have* can be either main verbs or auxiliaries.)

EXAMPLE: Recently many companies <u>have introduced</u> "pay-for-performance" plans.
                                                                         aux main

1. These plans offer financial incentives to workers based on production.

2. Some workers—but by no means all—are thrilled with the plans.

3. Many employees have been paid by the hour for years.

4. They can no longer depend on consistent paychecks.

5. However, some employees will be earning twice their regular salaries.

EXERCISE 4-3: Distinguishing between *sit/set, lie/lay,* and *rise/raise*

Compose six sentences, one each for the verbs *sit/set, lie/lay*, and *rise/raise*.

EXAMPLE: She *set* the vase on the table carefully.

1.

2.

3.

4.

5.

6.

EXERCISE 4-4: Understanding tense

Using complete sentences, fill in the verb-tense chart for the following verbs: *write, smile, go.*

Present:

Present perfect:

Present progressive:

Present perfect progressive:

Past:

Past perfect:

Past progressive:

Past perfect progressive:

Future:

Future perfect:

Future progressive:

Future perfect progressive:

EXERCISE 4-5: Using appropriate tenses

In the following sentences, write out the verb in parentheses in a tense appropriate to the meaning of the sentence.

EXAMPLE: Many people (study) _have studied_ the events that (make) _made_ Salem, Massachusetts infamous.

1. For a year before the girls in Salem Village (begin) _____ accusing local people of witchcraft, disputes over land boundaries (plague) _____ the town.

2. In 1691, the village (be) _____ without a minister for years, but when Samuel Parris (arrive) _____ he (proclaim) _____, "Before the year (be) _____ out, I (sweep) _____ the devil from your midst!"

3. In the winter of that year, while his daughter and his niece (study) _____ Scripture, they (begin) _____ to shake and scream.

4. By the time the doctor (arrive) _____, the girls (behave) _____ strangely for days.

5. His conclusion (be) _____ chilling: "The girls (be) _____ bewitched."

6. Thus an episode (begin) _____ that (baffle) _____ us now and (baffle) _____ others in years to come.

EXERCISE 4-6: Understanding tense sequences

For each of the following sentences, write out the appropriate tense of the verb in parentheses. Determine tense by considering the sequence of tenses in each sentence.

EXAMPLE: Since the space program began, seventeen American astronauts (die) <u>have died</u> in the line of duty.

1. When the space program was in its infancy, nobody (believe) _____ that so many astronauts would lose their lives.

2. However, if you consider the number of tests and missions in which astronauts (participate) _____ over the years, you (realize) _____ that the number (be) _____ actually quite small.

3. Of course, we all remember the Challenger disaster of 1986, when seven men and women (kill) _____.

4. Before final plans were made to memorialize the fallen astronauts, NASA officials (consider) _____ the issue for over a year.

Using Verbs   35

5. The Astronauts Memorial Space Mirror, a tribute to fallen astronauts, (be) _____ located on 13.5 acres of land at the John F. Kennedy Space Center.

6. At first the idea was to build a monument to the seven who (die) _____ on the Challenger, but then officials (decide) _____ that the memorial (honor) _____ all who (die) _____ in the line of duty.

7. Conceived by a Florida architect and designed by a San Francisco firm, the memorial (be) _____ a black granite mirror that (rise) _____ 42 feet into the air.

8. In order to create a sense of light, the names of the astronauts (carve) _____ right through the granite, so that sunlight (stream) _____ through the letters.

9. A computer program (allow) _____ the memorial to rotate and track the sun during daylight hours.

10. Like the Vietnam memorial in Washington, D.C., the "Space Mirror," as it (call) _____, (honor) _____ our dead for generations to come.

EXERCISE 4-7: Recognizing active and passive verbs

Rewrite the following paragraph in the space below, changing the italicized verbs from active to passive and vice versa, supplying subjects where necessary.

EXAMPLE: Rene Jules Dobos *was well known* as a bacteriologist and an environmentalist.

REVISION: People know Rene Jules Dobos as a bacteriologist and an environmentalist.

Although his early dreams involved athletic achievements, Dubos eventually *studied* agriculture. The young Dubos found microbiology and chemistry tedious because the subjects *were explored* by students in a laboratory setting. Later, after he *completed* doctoral studies in soil microbiology, he began working with pneumonia patients. It was through experiments based on his work that three researchers from the Rockefeller Institute for Medical Research *won* the Nobel Prize in Chemistry. Although Dubos was responsible for the first clinically useful antibiotic, known as gramacidin, he eventually concluded that ecology and not medicine *held out* the best hope for curing disease.

Using Verbs 37

EXERCISE 4-8: Using the subjunctive mood

In each of the following sentences, change the mood of the underlined verb if necessary. Circle the number of any correct sentences.

EXAMPLE: The rules of the equestrian sport of dressage require
wear
that a rider <u>wears</u> formal attire.

1. Many riders think, "If I <u>was</u> able to wear more comfortable clothing, I could ride better."

2. But the rules dictate that a rider <u>appears</u> in the arena wearing a jacket, breeches, and tall boots.

3. Some riders believe that more contemporary clothing would give observers a better sense of the athleticism that the sport <u>requires</u>.

4. Instead, a rider in the dressage arena must dress as though he or she <u>was</u> living at the turn of the century—the 19th century.

5. Despite the attractions of tradition, many riders who find themselves wearing a long-sleeved shirt and black jacket on a hot summer day think, "I wish I <u>was</u> wearing a T-shirt!"

EXERCISE 4-9: Review

Rewrite the following paragraph on a separate sheet of paper, correcting the use of verb form, tense, and mood. If passive sentences would be more effective as active (or vice versa), rewrite them.

Debate over the Civil Rights Bill of 1991 had focused on the concept of quotas. In the 1960s, they had implemented quotas in order to assure minority students' rights to higher education. But by the 1980s, the term "quota" became the equivalent of a four-letter word. Gains made by civil rights groups throughout the 1960s and early 1970s had been lost as the country continued its move to the right. White students argued, "If I would have been black, I'd have no trouble getting into college!" Visions of unqualified minority students displacing deserving white students were conjured up by politicians eager to harness the conservative vote. But in the late 1980s, the concept of quotas had been taking on a different look. Prestigious universities were admitting that for several years they have been using quotas to limit the number of Asian Americans on their campuses. And then someone discovered that universities such as Harvard, Stanford, and Yale are regularly accepting athletes whose qualifications will be lower than those of many rejected students. Furthermore, it was discovered that the group receiving preferential treatment more often than any other was not African Americans, Chicanos, Asian Americans, or any other minority group. Rather, the most preferred group has consisted of children of alumni—usually very white and very wealthy.

EXERCISE 4-10: Understanding verb use

Photocopy a brief passage from one of your textbooks, and analyze its use of verbs. First circle all of the verbs in the passage (count verb phrases as a single verb), and then identify the verbs by tense, voice, and mood. Finally, comment on the use of several auxiliaries in the passage. How do the various verb forms used contribute to the meaning of the selection?

CHAPTER 5

Correcting Errors in Subject-Verb Agreement

For use with Chapter 32 of *The Academic Writer's Handbook*

EXERCISE 5-1: Subject-verb agreement

In the following sentences, determine whether the subject is singular or plural, and underline the appropriate verb.

EXAMPLE: Heroes (<u>embody</u>/embodies) qualities valued in a given culture.

1. Everybody (has/have) a hero.

2. In some cultures, courage and bravery in battle (constitute/constitutes) heroic qualities.

3. Young people, whether they live in the United States or Europe, often (glorify/glorifies) rock performers.

4. The singer and performer (act/acts) as a role model for youth.

5. In religious ceremonies, the person who is able to overcome persecution at the hands of nonbelievers (is/are) often considered heroic.

6. The saint, along with other types of heroes, (become/becomes) the subject of legends.

7. Heroes are not always remembered throughout the ages; some (is/are) forgotten all too soon.

8. Every generation (has/have) heroes to admire.

9. Often members of the same generation of people (disagree/disagrees) about who is a hero.

10. The person who values action and adventure (admire/admires) one hero, while people who value contemplation and serenity (admire/admires) another.

11. Athletics (is/are) an area that (produce/produces) many heroes.

12. There (is/are) many reasons to admire a great athlete.

13. Training the body to perform strenuous feats (is/are) considered admirable.

14. *The Hero with a Thousand Faces* (is/are) Joseph Campbell's analysis of heroes in mythology.

15. No single hero or god (satisfy/satisfies) every person's requirements.

16. Some, however, (has/have) come close.

17. Their ability to help humans feel the presence of the divine (make/makes) Buddha, Jesus, and Mohammed heroes that have endured through the ages.

18. The cause of hero worship (is/are) people themselves.

19. Yes, people (is/are) the cause of hero worship.

20. To worship heroes (is/are) to be human.

Exercise 5-2: Subject-verb agreement

Correct any problems in subject-verb agreement in the following sentences.

EXAMPLE: Several lobbyists on Capitol Hill is trying to get that legislation passed.

REVISION: Several lobbyists on Capitol Hill are trying to get that legislation passed.

1. Politics, according to some pundits, make strange bedfellows.

2. There is three good arguments for voting against the referendum.

3. Each of those books have been made into a movie.

4. Neither Jason nor Madison were at the rally.

5. The Senate are getting ready to recess.

6. The report, along with the tables and graphs, are due on Tuesday.

7. The results of the latest poll indicates that the incumbent has a strong lead.

8. Either Paula or the other people in her group are building the Web site.

9. Reading mystery novels help to pass the winter evenings.

10. The Quarter Horse and the Thoroughbred is both popular breeds in the United States.

Exercise 5-3: Subject-verb agreement

Correct any problems in subject-verb agreement in the following sentences.

EXAMPLE: Do either of the candidates have anything new to say?

REVISION: Does either of the candidates have anything new to say?

1. One of the students who works with the seniors are setting up a bingo game for Friday night.

2. Despite advances, there is still too many people living below the poverty level.

3. Neither the lawyer nor his client were able to convince the jury.

4. Either of those abstracting services are a good source for articles on psychology.

5. A herd of ponies were grazing on the lawn.

6. Each of the guests are bringing a dish to the potluck party.

7. The only problem with this apartment are the neighbors.

8. Amanda, like her parents and her grandparents, love to ski.

9. The price of a pack of cigarettes have gone up tenfold in the past few decades.

10. There is two ways to interpret Nick's remark: literally or ironically.

Exercise 5-4: Subject-verb agreement

Correct any problems in subject-verb agreement in the following sentences.

EXAMPLE: Which one of the senators are sponsoring the bill?

REVISION: Which one of the senators is sponsoring the bill?

1. Which criteria is the most important one for ranking the printers?

2. To go to the Olympics are the dream of many athletes.

3. Measles are usually a childhood disease.

4. One of the biggest investments made by most people are buying a home.

5. *The Red Shoes* are about a ballet dancer.

6. The manager, as well as the employees, donate an hour to charity every week.

7. I had to tell my nephew that neither his baseball hat nor his T-shirt were appropriate for his job interview.

8. Classic children's books, such as *Black Beauty*, becomes popular again with each new generation.

9. The rudeness of the sales clerks were astounding.

10. North and South Carolina was hit by the hurricane.

CHAPTER 6

Using Adjectives and Adverbs

For use with Chapter 33 of *The Academic Writer's Handbook*

EXERCISE 6-1: Recognizing adjectives and adverbs

Make a photocopy of a brief passage from one of your textbooks. Circle the adjectives and adverbs and draw arrows to the words they modify. Explain how the adjectives enhance meaning.

EXERCISE 6-2: Using adjectives and adverbs

Add adjectives and adverbs to the sentences below to make them clearer and more lively. (Remember than adjectives and adverbs can be phrases and clauses as well as single words.)

EXAMPLE: Martin needed a change.

REVISION: *Weary* Martin *desperately* needed a *significant* change.

1. Martin planted a garden.

2. The plants grew.

3. Martin took a vacation.

4. Sherry looked after the garden.

5. Everything in the garden died.

EXERCISE 6-3: Distinguishing between adjectives and adverbs

In the following sentences, determine whether the modifier should be an adjective or an adverb. Then underline the appropriate modifier from the pairs of words in parentheses. (The first word in each pair is an adjective, the second an adverb.)

EXAMPLE: Micromachine technology is progressing quite (quick, <u>quickly</u>).

1. This kind of research had been conducted (previous, previously) in electronics laboratories.

2. The speed of developments from electronics to mechanics has been (startling, startlingly).

3. Micromachines will (sure, surely) be useful in medicine.

4. Researchers in the field are looking (excited, excitedly) to the future.

5. Researchers in the field are looking (excited, excitedly) about the future.

Using Adjectives and Adverbs   49

EXERCISE 6-4: Using *good/well* and *bad/badly*

In the following sentences, fill in the blank with *good* or *well*, *bad* or *badly*. Then draw an arrow from the word chosen to the word modified.

EXAMPLE: After the accident, Eleanor looked _bad_.

1. The fact that she drives _____ kept the accident from being more serious.

2. She certainly is a _____ driver.

3. Also, if she didn't smell so _____, she'd never have noticed the leaking gasoline.

4. She said that in the hospital everything tasted _____.

5. Regardless, after a few days she'll feel _____ again.

EXERCISE 6-5: Comparative and superlative forms

In the following sentences, correct any errors in comparative and superlative forms or other adjective forms.

EXAMPLE: Of the New York City Ballet and the Bolshoi, some consider the Bolshoi to be the ~~best~~ *better*.

1. When George Balanchine, the director of the New York City Ballet, died in 1983, he was succeeded by one of the most youngest directors ever to head a famous company.

2. The 4-H member's entry was one of the most perfect roses the judges had ever seen.

3. Chicken or fish is a good choice if you are looking for a more healthier alternative to higher-calorie protein sources.

4. Pizza is good, but I like calzones best.

5. Some of the photographs in his collection are extremely unique.

6. I didn't hardly know what to do when the computer deleted my files.

7. One of the most happiest times of his life was his early childhood.

8. Of your two writing samples, the report is the best.

9. The most liveliest presentation was given by the last group.

10. One of the most unique movies I saw last year was *The Cell*.

EXERCISE 6-6: Review

In the following paragraph, correct any errors in the use of adjectives and adverbs.

The term "third world" refers to those countries which don't belong neither to the first world of western capitalism nor to the second world of eastern communism. In terms of standard of living, the first world is considered the better. Both the first and second worlds, however, haven't had no trouble maintaining the most minimum standard of living for their populations. In the third world such is not the case. The citizens of third-world countries are the most poorly on the earth, even if some of them are governed by the most wealthiest individuals. Some theories blame third-world poverty on the industrial nations, while others cite factors within the third-world countries themselves. It is true that industrial nations don't seem to feel too badly when faced with the real deplorable conditions of life in much of the world's most poor countries. However, the multitude of internal problems—from overpopulation to underdevelopment—within third-world countries themselves also plays a role in their poverty.

Washington think-tank third-world research economists tend to favor the latter theories. Regardless of which is the valider theory, the difficultest economic problems facing the world today have their roots in the divisions between the third world and the rest of the world.

CHAPTER 7

Correcting Misplaced and Dangling Modifiers

For use with Chapter 34 of *The Academic Writer's Handbook*

EXERCISE 7-1: Misplaced and squinting modifiers

Rewrite the following sentences by repositioning misplaced and squinting modifiers or by recasting the sentence so that it reads clearly. (You can choose which word you want a squinting modifier to describe.) Circle the number of correct sentences.

EXAMPLE: Budgets for major motion pictures include provisions for advertising, which seem to be growing steadily.

REVISION: Budgets for major motion pictures, *which seem to be growing steadily*, include provisions for advertising.

1. Concentrating on producing the movie itself, considerations such as an advertising budget rarely concerned producers of the past.

2. Within the last two decades, producers who understood the business thoroughly approved budgets for marketing purposes.

3. Television seems to be the reason for the increasing importance of marketing campaigns, which dominates the leisure lives of many Americans.

4. An audiovisual medium itself, television provides the perfect advertising ground for movies.

5. Early movie advertising on television consisted of a voiceover and a shot of the movie's title, usually a deep male voice.

6. Marketing executives who recognized the value of television ads for movies clearly began to take advantage of the medium.

7. Consisting of a quick, exciting scene from an upcoming movie, producers make millions on movie "teasers."

8. Also called "trailers," people seem taken in by these vignettes.

9. Too many trailers can ruin business for a movie with exciting features.

10. Trailers themselves seem to have become entertainment for some people, taking on a life of their own.

EXERCISE 7-2: Limiting modifiers

Rewrite the following sentences, repositioning the limiting modifier to give the sentence a different meaning.

EXAMPLE: Birth order seems to be an important factor only in the development of some children.

REVISION: Birth order *only* seems to be an important factor in the development of some children.

1. Just where you are in relation to your siblings can have an effect on your personality.

2. Psychologists say that birth order is almost as important as parent-child bonding to all children.

3. Even amateurs can trace some of their personality characteristics to birth order.

4. The eldest, for example, is always a person who takes responsibility seriously.

5. Simply being the youngest can make a person dependent on everyone.

EXERCISE 7-3: Repositioning modifiers

Rewrite the following sentences, repositioning modifiers so that there are clear links between subjects, verbs, and objects or complements. Circle the number of any correct sentences.

EXAMPLE: When Graham Greene died in 1991, he over the course of his life had written more than fifty books.

REVISION: When Graham Greene died in 1991, he had written more than fifty books *over the course of his life.*

1. Greene's writing was to the public that bought over twenty million copies of his books the work of a master storyteller.

2. Most novelists write, according to literary and popular culture critics, either "serious" literature or "escape" literature.

3. Greene's writing included, much to the chagrin of narrow-minded literary scholars, both types of literature.

4. The writer, Greene remarked on a number of occasions, should not be ashamed of being popular among non-academics.

5. Greene was, as a young child and even as a young man, occasionally suicidal.

6. He, in 1920, at the age of 16, underwent psychoanalysis.

7. In 1925, because he was engaged to marry a Catholic, Greene converted to Catholicism.

8. Catholic theology provided because of its concepts of sin and salvation Greene with the central theme for most of his work.

9. Greene won with his adventure story that also explored the notion of redemption both critical and popular acclaim.

10. He was, in the eyes of most literary critics, one of the great voices of the 20th century.

EXERCISE 7-4: Repairing dangling modifiers

Rewrite the following sentences, repairing the dangling modifiers by revising the sentence to restore the word modified. Circle the number of any sentences that are correct.

EXAMPLE: Responding to medical advice about healthy diets, fish is being eaten more and more these days.

REVISION: Responding to medical advice about healthy diets, people are eating fish more and more these days.

1. Searching for the perfect seafood dinner, haddock is a good choice.

2. With its mild flavor and smooth texture, there is good reason for the demand.

3. Discouraged by high costs and poor catches, commercial fishing has been abandoned in many coastal areas.

4. More efficient and more profitable, "fish farming" is slowly replacing commercial fishing.

5. Like animals raised on farms, a number of chemicals are injected.

Correcting Misplaced and Dangling Modifiers

EXERCISE 7-5: Misplaced and dangling modifiers

Rewrite the following paragraph, revising sentences to eliminate misplaced and dangling modifiers.

EXAMPLE: Soaring effortlessly through the air, people have always envied birds.

REVISION: People have always envied birds, soaring effortlessly through the air.

Inventors were, centuries before Wilbur and Orville Wright first left the ground in Kitty Hawk, imagining ways in which people could fly. But the fascination didn't end with the advent of commercial air flight. Hang gliders became in the '70s the rage, and now the latest fad for would-be fliers is bungee jumping. Bungee jumping, apparently originating in Europe and Australia, combines the thrill of flight with the adventure of parachuting. Jumpers attach themselves to a strong cord, usually made of rubber, and then freefall. Reaching speeds of up to 60 m.p.h. and falling sometimes 100 feet, a "high" that not many people can tolerate is experienced. Bungee jumpers had to at first avoid police, because their favorite jumping spot, bridges, were off limits according to the law. Now more legal spots for jumping are appearing, among them a 140-foot tower in Colorado. And one of the most popular spots from which to jump is itself airborne—a hot air balloon. People who jump often describe the experience as exhilarating.

EXERCISE 7-6: Revising

Look through your graded papers to find instructors' comments regarding misplaced or dangling modifiers. Reread the papers, identify the errors as you read by using the strategies outlined in this chapter. Then revise the errors. (If you don't have any graded papers handy, look through any body of writing you've done recently.)

CHAPTER 8

Using Nouns and Pronouns

For use with Chapter 35 of *The Academic Writer's Handbook*

EXERCISE 8-1: Using pronoun forms

Fill in the blanks in the following sentences with the appropriate form of the pronoun in parentheses.

EXAMPLE: In 1966, the Surgeon General announced that cigarettes were harmful to health. Many smokers who heard (he) *him* making the announcement now knew that the habit was deadly.

1. Friends and families of smokers asked (they) _____ to quit.

2. Twenty years after the first announcement, smokers were told, "(you) _____ smoking also endangers everyone in your vicinity."

3. "It's horrible to realize that it was (I) _____ who was responsible for the health problems of my children," reported one smoker.

4. As pressure to ban smoking in public places grew, some smokers fought back, protesting, "(we) _____ smokers have rights too!"

5. In the new health-conscious climate, however, (they) _____ was a cause that was decidedly unpopular.

6. Children asked their parents, "How can you jeopardize the health of your children, (we) _____ who depend on you?"

7. Co-workers complained that it was (they) _____, not the smokers, (who) _____ rights were being violated.

8. Smokers countered with claims of discrimination: "Society is treating (we) _____ smokers as second-class citizens!"

9. Gradually, over the objections of many smokers, demands to restrict (they) _____ smoking to certain areas were met, creating what are now known as "smoke-free zones."

10. Nonsmokers told smokers that (they) _____ and (they) _____ habit were unwelcome in public places.

EXERCISE 8-2: Recognizing pronoun forms

Underline all of the pronouns in the following paragraph, and above each identify the case with the abbreviation *s*—subjective, *o*—objective, or *p*—possessive.

EXAMPLE: Although many smokers were able to kick the habit,
                            s   *p*
<u>they</u> soon discovered that quitting smoking had <u>its</u>

own problems.

Many smokers discovered that quitting made them irritable, causing problems at work and at home. Their job performance suffered, and spouses and children found that a reformed smoker isn't always a joy to her family. Said the son of one reformed smoker, "Sometimes I want to give her a cigarette just to have a little peace in the house!" Other smokers faced yet another problem in the search to curb their desire for nicotine. A man who quit smoking after fifteen years put it this way: "You think your problems are over now that you have quit, but the craving doesn't leave you alone. So you eat—and put on weight." Studies have shown that people who quit smoking do in fact gain weight, some of them as much as 30 pounds. Researchers warn us, however, that while smoking certainly plays its part in curbing our appetites, the health risks of excess weight cannot compare to the health risks of smoking.

EXERCISE 8-3: Using appropriate forms of *who* and related pronouns

Fill in the blanks in the following sentences with the appropriate forms of the pronouns *whose, who, whom, whoever,* and *whomever.*

EXAMPLE: The class was studying a poet _whose_ works were well known.

1. The Robert Frost poem opens with these words: "_____ woods these are I think I know."

2. Reading Frost's lines to the class, the professor asked if anyone could describe the person _____ was speaking in the poem.

3. "_____ it was, he sure loved the woods!" came one reply.

4. The professor then asked the class, "_____ is the speaker addressing in this poem?"

5. A bored student whispered, "_____ he's talking to, my only answer is '_____ cares?'"

EXERCISE 8-4: Understanding pronoun use

Photocopy a brief passage that contains a number of pronouns from one of your textbooks. Circle all of the pronouns, and then list them. Using what you've learned about case and function so far, identify the pronouns by case and explain their function in the sentence.

CHAPTER 9

Correcting Errors in Pronoun-Antecedent Agreement and Reference

For use with Chapter 36 of *The Academic Writer's Handbook*

EXERCISE 9-1: Pronoun-antecedent agreement with collective nouns

In the following sentences, determine whether the collective noun has a singular or a plural meaning, and underline the appropriate pronoun.

EXAMPLE: The team was about to lose (<u>its</u>, their) fourth game in a row.

1. After the loss, the team bickered among (itself, themselves).

2. The crowd booed heartily, expressing (its, their) disapproval.

3. A Brownie troop could have forged (its, their) way around the field more effectively than the team.

4. The press corps shook (its, their) heads in disbelief.

5. A couple who had both bet against the team happily collected (its, their) winnings.

EXERCISE 9-2: Using gender-appropriate pronouns

In the following sentences, replace gender-specific pronouns by using any of the five conventions listed in the chapter. Remember to change other elements in the sentence as needed.

EXAMPLE:
he or she
When ~~he~~ enters an urban office building, the average person is drawn into a bustling world of activity. (Or: "When *entering* . . .")

1. A receptionist is busy tending to her telephone, while a security guard walks his lobby beat.

2. Once in the heart of the building, the visitor sees a businessman making his deals and a secretary typing her letters.

3. The world of business keeps a person constantly on his guard.

4. Often an attorney is involved with business deals, offering his best legal advice.

5. When the papers are signed, it's time for the file clerk to do her job and file the documents.

Correcting Pronoun-Antecedent Agreement and Reference 69

EXERCISE 9-3: Correcting faulty pronoun reference

Check the following sentences for clear pronoun reference. If pronoun reference is unclear, then replace pronouns with nouns or move pronouns closer to their antecedents. Circle the number of any correct sentences.

EXAMPLE: Upton Sinclair's novel *The Jungle* was published in 1906, the same year that Samuel Hopkins Adams's *Great American Fraud* was published. ~~He~~ Sinclair also published several other books, among them *Oil!* and *Boston*.

1. Sinclair wrote *The Jungle* to expose corruption in Chicago's meat packing industry, especially mistreatment of workers and unsanitary conditions. It became very well known.

2. Sinclair was one of a group of writers active primarily in the cities of pre-World War I United States who questioned the morality of the capitalist system.

3. The term "muckraker" was coined by Theodore Roosevelt and applied to writers like Sinclair because of the nature of their writing, which refers to a line from John Bunyan's *Pilgrim's Progress*.

4. The muckrakers were at odds with industrialists and many politicians. They didn't approve of their methods for making money.

5. In part as a result of the muckrakers' work, the Beef Inspection Act was passed. It curbed abuses in the industry.

Correcting Pronoun-Antecedent Agreement and Reference

EXERCISE 9-4: Correcting faulty pronoun reference

Check the following sentences for problems with stating pronoun reference directly. Revise by providing direct antecedents for pronouns; making sure that pronouns don't refer to possessive nouns; and making sure that relative pronouns and the pronouns *it*, *they*, and *you* are used appropriately. Circle the number of any correct sentences.

EXAMPLE: Organizations ranging from the National Institute of Child Health to the American Cancer Society have warned about the dangers of excessive alcohol consumption. ~~This has~~ *These warnings have* resulted in heightened awareness of alcohol abuse.

1. People's attitudes toward alcohol are ambivalent. They understand the dangers, but they live in a society that glorifies drinking.

2. You can drink moderately with no risk to your health, but you should avoid heavy drinking.

3. Health officials are determined to educate people, and it seems to be having some effect.

4. Even liquor companies, that depend on the use of alcohol for their profits, are beginning to preach moderation.

5. It was not too long ago that some people praised alcohol because it was a remedy for many ills.

6. The Surgeon General's Office, who are the watchdogs of the nation's health, has issued warnings about alcohol use during pregnancy.

7. Since a pregnant woman's fetus can be irreparably harmed by alcohol, she is better off abstaining for the duration of the pregnancy.

8. Alcohol is not harmful if used moderately; thus it is not considered dangerous to the entire population.

9. They conclude that one drink per day is not dangerous for the average person.

10. Drunk driving is responsible for half of the fatal automobile accidents in this country, more than half of fire deaths, and a significant proportion of drownings, home accidents, and violent crimes as well, which means that alcohol is surely a dangerous drug.

Correcting Pronoun-Antecedent Agreement and Reference 73

EXERCISE 9-5: Recognizing clear pronoun reference

Photocopy several paragraphs from one of your textbooks. Try to find a passage that narrates an event: a scientist's discovery, an historical figure's accomplishments, or a section of a short story or novel. Circle all of the pronouns in the section, and draw arrows to their antecedents. Then, answer the following questions: How frequently does the writer keep pronouns close to their antecedents? If there are cases in which the two are separated by long phrases or clauses, is the pronoun reference still clear? If your answer is "no" for any parts of the passage, rewrite those parts to make the reference clearer.

EXERCISE 9-6: Review

Revise the following paragraph by correcting errors in subject-verb and pronoun-antecedent agreement. Eliminate any inappropriate gender reference as well.

In the past twenty years, consumers have become more and more aware of the environment. After World War II, this society became not only a consumer society but they became a disposable society as well. A person used paper plates and plastic flatware when eating his dinner, and cleaned up afterward with paper towels. Consumers bought health and beauty aids packaged in layers of plastic and cardboard. Babies wore disposable diapers, and parents wiped his or her bottom with disposable cloths. If an alien had landed anywhere in the United States during the middle part of this century, they would have considered us the most wasteful people on earth—and we probably were. The earth was being polluted, and the cause of the pollution were people. After Earth Day in 1970, however, we began to change all that. Now bottles, cans, and paper is recycled. We check the ingredients on a can to see if it's dangerous to the earth. We fertilize our lawns with organic material rather than chemicals, and we forswear use of disposable items. What are the consequences of our environmental awareness? Many results are heartening, but some results of this new environmentalism are bad. Each of the environmental groups has their own goals, some of them conflicting. In addition, the ordinary citizen—as well as the educated environmentalist—sometimes thinks that the problem is solved. There are many dangers here, primary among them a tendency toward complacency. This planet, with her magnificent oceans, majestic forests, and solemn deserts, needs our full attention now.

EXERCISE 9-7: Revising

Look through your graded papers to find instructors' comments regarding unclear pronoun reference. Reread the papers, identifying the errors as you read by using the strategies outlined in this chapter. Then revise the errors. (If you don't have any graded papers handy, look through any body of writing you've done recently.)

CHAPTER 10

Correcting Errors in Consistency

For use with Chapter 37 of *The Academic Writer's Handbook*

EXERCISE 10-1: Correcting shifts

Rewrite each of the following sentences to correct shifts in person, number, tense, mood, or voice. (There is more than one way to correct some of the sentences.) Circle the number of any correct sentences.

EXAMPLE: Universities in the United States receive government funding, for which ~~you~~ *they* provide information on research costs and "indirect costs."

1. If a university received funds, it must provide a clear accounting of how it spent those funds.

2. Universities are granted funds by government agencies for scientific research and development; when you apply, you estimate what your "indirect costs" will be.

3. What are indirect costs? They are any costs not directly related to the research itself; it includes administration, maintenance, and libraries.

4. For example, if a university were to apply for a grant from the Defense Department, it estimates not only the costs incurred by conducting the research, but general costs involved in operating the university as well.

5. Some people prefer to call indirect costs "overhead," while they are called "padding" by skeptical observers.

6. The government agency granting the funds is supposed to oversee the disbursement; you do this by auditing the university's overhead charges.

7. If any discrepancies emerge during the audit, they are to be reconciled before additional funds are dispersed.

8. During the 1980s, Stanford University received major funding from the Office of Naval Research; not only did it fail to report overhead costs adequately, but they apparently used some of the funds on things like yachts and flowers.

9. When the Stanford story broke, many observers had blamed the hopelessly confused regulations involved in university research.

10. The Stanford incident resulted in stricter guidelines for accountability of indirect costs.

EXERCISE 10-2: Correcting shifts

Rewrite the following sentences, correcting shifts in tone, number, tense, mood, voice or the use of direct or indirect discourse. Circle the number of any correct sentences.

EXAMPLE: Scientists have always had a heck of a time studying gamma rays because the earth's atmosphere shields it from most of the rays.

REVISION: Scientists have always had <u>difficulty</u> studying gamma rays because the earth's atmosphere shields it from most of the rays.

1. Tennis elbow is when the tendons of your arm are irritated or inflamed.

2. The town's recycling bins are not being emptied often enough, resulting in a really gross mess.

3. Everyone who gives a presentation on Thursday will have them videotaped.

4. The President said I will not veto the bill.

5. If he were to win the election, it will change the dynamics of the state legislature.

6. The writer has an absolutely awesome ability to portray the conflicts between several generations of women.

7. The narrator of *Rebecca* is never given a first name; she was referred to only as "the second Mrs. de Winter."

8. When removing old wallpaper, first score the paper with a perforating tool, then it is necessary to use a plant sprayer to apply a wallpaper-removing solution.

9. A photovoltaic system is where you get electricity from the sun.

10. A veterinarian from the Maryland Department of Health said I don't think we should be overly concerned about the West Nile Virus.

EXERCISE 10-3: Correcting mixed constructions

Rewrite each of the following sentences in two ways to eliminate mixed constructions and faulty predication. Circle the number of any correct sentences.

EXAMPLE: Psychotherapy is where an analyst and a patient delve into the patient's past to help explain and control behavior.

REVISION 1: Psychotherapy is a clinical situation in which an analyst and a patient delve into the patient's past to help explain and control behavior.

REVISION 2: In psychotherapy, an analyst and a patient delve into the patient's past to help explain and control behavior.

1. When psychotherapy is a success means that the patient trusts the analyst.

2. By undergoing analysis can help many troubled individuals overcome anxiety.

3. Because of the success of psychoanalytic theory is responsible for the popularity of psychotherapy in past years.

4. One reason for the recent decline in the popularity of psychotherapy is because of the rigidity of its rules.

5. The fact that few patients can benefit from psychotherapy, and the process is a long one.

6. Although psychotherapy is no longer as popular as in the past, but some people still swear by its benefits.

7. Group therapy is when a single analyst works with several patients at once.

8. The evolution of psychotherapy is interested in serving a complex society.

9. Rather than abandon psychotherapy completely, many analysts have adapted it.

10. In discussing psychotherapy is recognized as a significant but limited success.

EXERCISE 10-4: Editing Elliptical Constructions

Rewrite the following sentences to correct problems with elliptical constructions and comparisons. Circle the number of any correct sentences.

EXAMPLE: Audiences always had great respect and faith in Leonard Bernstein.

REVISION: Audience always had great respect <u>for</u> and faith in Leonard Bernstein.

1. Audiences in the United States loved Bernstein better than other composers.

2. Many consider Bernstein is the greatest American composer to date.

3. Bernstein's conducting style was flamboyant, and his scores lively.

4. Traditional conducting was far more formal than Bernstein.

5. His devotion and belief in children led him to conduct many "Young People's Concerts."

6. Bernstein began playing piano at age ten, and orchestras at twenty-three.

7. Critics have said his genius was legendary.

8. His compositions were often more daring than those of his contemporaries.

9. Some of his later works were not as popular.

10. Bernstein will be remembered more for his popular work, especially *West Side Story*.

EXERCISE 10-5: Review

Rewrite the following paragraph, revising sentences to eliminate shifts, mixed constructions, and incomplete sentences.

      The cost of medical care in the United States has become the subject of more intense debate. A system that in the past was capable of providing the best care in the world will now be in danger of collapse. Among the issues involved in this debate are

Medicaid and Medicare costs, the financial situation of hospitals, and escalating health insurance premiums. Since both state and federal governments are not in good financial shape is the reason why Medicaid and Medicare payments to care providers are shrinking. And those payments are only trickling in. Someone who has been dropped from the Medicaid rolls still needs medical care, and some of them very expensive care. These people all end up as nonpaying patients in county or city hospitals; it's foolish to consider such patients aren't a burden on the community. In addition, the costs of doing business, along with increased malpractice insurance rates, have sent hospital finances into a tailspin. (But increases in malpractice premiums are a problem for doctors, too.) Add to this group insurance premiums that strain the costs of management and employees alike, and what you have is a health care crisis of major proportions.

EXERCISE 10-6: Recognizing consistency

Photocopy a brief passage from one of your textbooks, and pay close attention to the sequencing of tenses, consistency of mood, the use of voice, and the consistency and completeness of sentences. Answer the following questions in the space below: How does the writer's use of verbs help the reader understand the passage? How effectively are comparisons presented? How does the author handle elliptical constructions? Are there any apparent inconsistencies (in voice, for example)? If so, can you explain why the writer may have chosen this shift?

EXERCISE 10-7: Review

Look through your graded papers to find instructors' comments regarding shifts and/or mixed constructions. Reread the papers, identifying the specific types of problems and revising accordingly. (If you don't have any graded papers handy, look through any body of writing you've done recently.)

CHAPTER 11

Correcting Faulty Parallelism

For use with Chapter 38 of *The Academic Writer's Handbook*

EXERCISE 11-1: Eliminating faulty parallelism

Rewrite the following sentences, eliminating faulty parallelism. (While some sentences may be correct, they can be improved with parallel structure.) Circle the number of any correct sentences.

EXAMPLE: In mid-19th-century New England, the Transcendentalists flourished, publishing a magazine, teaching schoolchildren, and they tried to set up an ideal community.

REVISION: In mid-19th-century New England, the Transcendentalists flourished, publishing a magazine, teaching schoolchildren, and trying to set up an ideal community.

1. The Transcendentalists supported both abolition and for women to have equal rights.

2. Among the most famous Transcendentalists were Bronson Alcott, whose daughter Louisa May became a famous novelist, and Ralph Waldo Emerson, writing great essays and delivering powerful lectures.

3. Transcendentalism did not offer any clear set of beliefs; rather, it was suggesting a way to view the world.

4. While traditional Christianity believed that divine intervention was necessary to improve human nature, for the Transcendentalists humanity could be improved by relying on its own strength.

5. Transcendentalism was an offshoot of Unitarianism, which had rejected Calvinism and liberal beliefs were embraced by them.

6. Those who joined the Transcendentalists were often ministers and people who wrote for a living.

7. Margaret Fuller's contribution to Transcendentalism included editing the magazine *The Dial*, and she also conducted discussions for women.

8. Brook Farm, an experiment in communal living, was established both to help support the group and educate children.

9. The more literary members of the group included poets, novelists, and lecturers.

10. Perhaps the greatest legacy of Transcendentalism is not its religious or philosophical belief, but how it influenced great literature.

EXERCISE 11-2: Creating parallel structures

Correct each sentence below so that it has parallel structure.

EXAMPLE: The horses need to be groomed, watered, fed, and clean their stalls.

REVISION: The horses need to be groomed, watered, and fed, and to have their stalls cleaned.

1. The price for a flight to Acapulco is much less than Bermuda.

2. When you become familiar with a search engine, the more you can use it efficiently.

3. The library neither will reserve books nor will check them out within five minutes of closing.

4. In preparing a family history, look both at family documents such as Bibles, letters, diaries, and Internet sites on genealogy.

5. Scrub the area with peroxide, iodine, alcohol, and then apply a compress and bandage.

6. For their vacation, they will either go to Scotland or Ireland.

7. The *Miranda v. Arizona* case requires police to inform suspects of the right to remain silent, any statements they make can be used against them, and an attorney will be provided if they cannot afford to pay.

8. U.S. Customs restricts travelers from bringing in certain animals, plants, medications, foods, and children may not bring in alcohol.

9. Either keep your radio turned down, or maybe you could wear headphones.

10. A well-designed Web page does not contain graphics that require excessive downloading time or reading unusual, difficult-to-read fonts.

EXERCISE 11-3: Creating parallel structures.

Correct each sentence below so that it has parallel structure.

EXAMPLE: Students in the work-study program can either register for their courses now or after they have their work schedules.

REVISION: Students in the work-study program can register for their courses either now or after they have their work schedules.

1. Using the Format menu, you can change the font, change line or paragraph spacing, and borders can also be added.

2. It's not safe for children to play in, around, or stand on the recycling containers.

3. The new software will enable teachers to perform several tasks:
   - keep a running total of each student's test scores
   - the average of each student's test scores
   - factoring in attendance as part of the final grade
   - calculate each student's class standing throughout the semester

4. Many speakers are using presentation software because it makes their presentations more professional looking, and also enabling them to import spreadsheets and graphics from other programs.

5. A high-protein diet allows the dieter to eat unlimited amounts of meat, but eating very little in the way of vegetables or starches.

6. When elderly people fall and injure themselves, the fear of falling again can lead to drastic changes in lifestyle and attitude, including they might be afraid to leave the house during bad weather or engaging in simple physical activities like walking.

7. The baby boomer generation consists of people born between 1946 and 1964, and grew up in an era of unprecedented prosperity.

8. There are three types of bacterial cells: rodlike, spiral, and some are shaped like spheres.

9. A Bactrian camel has two humps, a dromedary camel having only one; the hump is formed of muscle and fat with no bone, and changing shape depending on how much food and water the camel has had.

10. James Bond embodies the ideal playboy of the 1950s and 1960s: tough, sophisticated, and women can't resist him.

EXERCISE 11-4: Creating parallel structures

Study the paragraph by Abraham Lincoln below. Write an imitation of Lincoln's paragraph, beginning with one of the following sentences (or choose your own):

>A teenage marriage cannot last.
>A great concert can revitalize the soul.
>A child born in the ghetto will never be free.

A house divided against itself cannot stand. I believe this government cannot endure permanently half slave and half free. I do not expect the Union to be dissolved; I do not expect the house to fall; but I do expect it will cease to be divided. It will become all one thing, or all the other.

EXERCISE 11-5: Creating parallel structures

Rewrite the following outline, keeping elements at the same level of generality in parallel form.

Section Title: Preparing for surgery

    A.   Doctor takes a medical history

    B.   Blood tests by lab technician

    C.   Anesthesiologist—explaining procedure, asking questions

    D.   "Prep" undertaken by nursing staff

        1.   Any hair in immediate area shaved off

        2.   They thoroughly clean area

        3.   Isolation of area

Correcting Faulty Parallelism 95

EXERCISE 11-6: Recognizing parallel structures

Photocopy a page or two from one of your textbooks, and underline all parallel words, phrases, and clauses. Rewrite a couple of the sentences, eliminating the parallel structure. Compare the two: How does the use of parallelism contribute to the meaning of the passage? How does it affect the style of the piece? Write your responses below.

EXERCISE 11-7: Revising

As you revise drafts of any papers you're working on at present, look for places where parallel structure would make the paper more effective. It may be a series of words, or two phrases or clauses, or even a pair of sentences. Occasionally, a paragraph can be arranged around parallel structures (as in Exercise 11-4).

CHAPTER 12

Being Clear, Concise, and Direct

For use with Chapter 39 of *The Academic Writer's Handbook*

EXERCISE 12-1: Eliminating wordiness

Rewrite the following sentences, eliminating wordiness by combining sentences, reducing clauses and phrases to single words, and deleting unnecessary expletives (e.g., *It is, There are*). Circle the number of any correct sentences.

EXAMPLE: At the present time, many babies who are born prematurely can be saved.

REVISION: <u>Today</u>, many <u>premature</u> babies can be saved.

1. There are many babies who would have died within hours of birth ten years ago, but who live healthy lives today.

2. Babies do not have to wait until birth to be treated for some conditions. Even before birth, babies can be treated for some conditions.

3. Doctors can perform surgery on fetuses who are as young as 24 weeks.

4. Premature babies have many problems. Premature babies frequently suffer from developmental problems.

5. An unspecified number of babies need therapy to overcome disabilities.

6. Hydrotherapy involves working with children in water to improve motor skills.

7. Speech/communication therapy involves working with children's abilities to verbalize and use words.

8. There are entire families of disabled children that can sometimes benefit from therapy.

9. It is often the demands of a disabled child that can disrupt normal family life.

10. When the entire family is involved in the therapy for the disabled child, the life of the family runs more smoothly.

EXERCISE 12-2: Eliminating wordiness

Rewrite the following sentences, eliminating wordiness by changing passive verbs to active, replacing *be* and *have*, and revising nouns derived from verbs. Circle the number of any correct sentences.

EXAMPLE: In May 1935, two recovering alcoholics had a meeting to try to help one another overcome their dependence on alcohol.

REVISION: In May 1935, two recovering alcoholics <u>met</u> to try to help one another overcome their dependence on alcohol.

1. William Griffith Wilson and Robert Holbrook Smith gave support to each other as the two made attempts to lead sober lives.

2. Their experience was so successful that *Alcoholics Anonymous* was written by them in 1939, marking the beginning of the organization.

3. Alcoholics Anonymous is an organization that provides recovering alcoholics with the kind of support Wilson and Smith provided each other.

4. Current AA membership is about a million.

5. Spiritual values are stressed by AA, often mentioning God by name.

6. Recently other groups have sprung up in the belief that religion need not be a part of the recovery process.

7. The new groups, such as the Secular Organization for Sobriety (SOS), give emphasis to the alcoholic's own will power rather than the intervention of a higher power.

8. A group created especially for women alcoholics, Women for Sobriety (WFS) is an organization that has a focus on female alcoholics.

9. Another group, Rational Recovery (RR), emphasizes the power that the individual has to overcome alcoholism.

10. People are helped to maintain sobriety by all of these groups.

EXERCISE 12-3: Revising for clarity and conciseness

Revise the following sentences for greater clarity and conciseness.

EXAMPLE: The city enactment of an anti-smoking ordinance has caused a number of problems for restaurant owners who are attempting to comply with the ordinance before the deadline next week.

REVISION: Many restaurant owners are having problems meeting next week's deadline for complying with the city's new anti-smoking ordinance.

1. The lawyer told the reporters the verdict can only be decided by the jury.

2. I was completely fascinated by certain aspects of the registration process.

3. Frank Lloyd Wright took an approach to architecture that was innovative because it combined technological aspects into aesthetic things.

4. It is wise to consult a lawyer when preparing a will, but it is not required.

5. When you apply for your visa, you will need to provide details about your plans for traveling, including details about your flight number and the date you plan to depart.

6. There were a number of factors that affected the election outcome, including a low voter turnout in key precincts and poor weather conditions.

7. The virus that causes hepatitis can be spread by direct contact or indirect contact with a person who is infected.

8. I have read differing and conflicting opinions over the question of whether or not the poinsettia plant is toxic.

9. The preparation of a résumé that is suitable for scanning requires the writer to follow specific guidelines for the use of certain things like boldface and italics.

10. A cantilever is an item that is a horizontal projection and that has a support only at one end.

EXERCISE 12-4: Revising for clarity and conciseness

Revise the following sentences for greater clarity and conciseness.

EXAMPLE: In view of the fact that the university will not be holding classes next Monday, it will be necessary for students to hand in their papers on Friday.

REVISION: Since university classes are canceled next Monday, students should hand in their papers on Friday.

1. When you are in the process of painting cabinets, it is a tedious and time-consuming process to remove all the hardware before you begin painting, but you will be glad you did when you see the final results.

2. At the present point in time, there are two possible alternatives for us to take: continue on our present course of action or diversify into a new market.

3. In the event that I am unable to attend the meeting, I will send a representative in my place.

4. Due to the fact that it was founded in Detroit, which is known as the "Motor Town," Berry Gordy, Jr., named his company Motown Records.

5. The term "lost generation" is a term that was originated by a remark made by Gertrude Stein to Ernest Hemingway.
6. In 1963, New Hampshire became the state that was the first to adopt a lottery since 1894.
7. Lourdes, which is in southwestern France, is visited annually by about three million pilgrims a year who hope to be cured by the spring water there.
8. The disorder called Lyme disease, which is named after the town of Lyme, Connecticut, which is the place where it was first observed, is characterized in its early stage by a "bull's eye" rash.
9. Lamarck, unlike Darwin, thought that those changes that an animal undergoes during the course of its lifetime could be passed on to the next generation of its offspring.
10. I contacted him via phone with respect to the fact that he had not yet sent in his letters of recommendation.

EXERCISE 12-5: Review

Rewrite the following paragraph, eliminating wordiness with the techniques discussed in this chapter.

In 1954, a decision that would shake the nation was handed down by the Supreme Court in the case of *Brown v. Board of Education of Topeka*. There are many people who have some familiarity with the case that declared segregation in public schools unconstitutional. Not many, however, are knowledgeable about the fact that Thurgood Marshall was in point of fact the attorney who argued the case before the Supreme Court. In part as a result of this victory, and because he had succeeded in winning the case, President Lyndon Johnson appointed Marshall to the Supreme Court thirteen years later. The first black African American to sit on the high court, Marshall was born in Baltimore and received his education at Howard University Law School. As the legal director of the NAACP, Marshall was the one who brought to the Supreme Court many cases in addition to *Brown*. From 1938 to 1958, he argued more than thirty cases before the high court, winning all but three. Many of the cases he argued basically set in motion the machinery that continues to eliminate segregation at the present time. When he was appointed to the Supreme Court, Marshall vowed to give interpretations of the Constitution in terms of the promises it makes to protect the weakest, least powerful members of society. Marshall voted with the liberal majority of the court during the last final years of Chief Justice Earl Warren's tenure. As the court took on a tone that was more conservative, Marshall wrote many opinions that were dissenting in civil liberties cases. When William Brennan retired from the Supreme Court in 1990, Marshall was in a position that found himself isolated. A year after that point in time, as his health deteriorated and got worse, Marshall made the announcement of his resignation from the Court, ending an era of activism on behalf of civil rights that changed the country and made it a different place.

EXERCISE 12-6: Recognizing concise, clear, and direct prose

Photocopy an essay from a popular magazine such as *Time* or *Newsweek* (essays are usually on the last page of those two magazines). First, circle all of the verbs. How many are passive? Why do you suppose the writer made those verbs passive? Would any have been more effective in the active voice? How many instances can you find of *be* or *have* used as main verbs? Are those verbs necessary, or could any of them have been replaced by more active verbs? Then underline all of the nouns derived from verbs. Could any of these have been recast as verbs? Why do you suppose the writer chose to keep them as nouns? Finally, how do strong verbs contribute to the effect of the passage?

EXERCISE 12-7: Revising

As you revise drafts of papers you're working on at present, concentrate on conciseness, clarity, and directness. Try to identify the specific kinds of problems you have in this area so that you can look out for them in future drafts. Now compare your revisions to the originals: How much shorter are the revisions? How much clearer?

CHAPTER 13

Building Emphasis with Coordination and Subordination

For use with Chapter 40 of *The Academic Writer's Handbook*

EXERCISE 13-1: Creating equal emphasis

Using coordinating conjunctions, correlative conjunctions, and conjunctive adverbs, combine the following sentences to achieve equal emphasis.

EXAMPLE: A woman in England was bitten by a snake hidden in her Christmas tree. She plans to buy an artificial tree next year.

REVISION: A woman in England was bitten by a snake hidden in her Christmas tree; not surprisingly, she plans to buy an artificial tree next year.

1. Garnishment involves taking money owed to a person by one party to pay off that person's debt to a different party. The IRS may take money from a person's paycheck to pay off a debt owed to the IRS.

2. A protagonist is the main character in a story. An antagonist is an adversary.

3. A mild vitamin C deficiency may lead to joint tenderness and dental problems. A severe one may result in anemia or scurvy.

4. Civilians salute the flag by removing their hats, standing at attention, and placing their right hands over their hearts. Uniformed military personnel give a military salute.

5. Monosodium glutamate is a flavor enhancer. Many people have an adverse reaction to it, such as headache.

6. The statue known as the Colossus of Rhodes appeared to straddle the harbor. It was actually built on a promontory that overlooked the harbor.

7. Smoking, like cold, constricts blood vessels. A frostbite victim should not be allowed to smoke.

8. A baked potato has 93 calories. The same amount of French fries has 274 calories.

9. Few people write personal letters these days. Those that we receive are treasured.

10. Sulfites can cause asthmatic attacks. They destroy vitamin B.

Building Emphasis with Coordination and Subordination 111

EXERCISE 13-2: Achieving emphasis with dependent clauses

Combine the following pairs of sentences by converting one in each pair into a dependent clause.

EXAMPLE: The Industrial Revolution brought people into factories. At an earlier time, people's work and home lives were intertwined.

REVISION: Before the Industrial Revolution brought people into factories, their work and home lives were intertwined.

1. Work began to be concentrated in factories. At this point, the time people spent on the job became time spent away from the family.

2. Time spent on the job began to take precedence. The reason for this was that the worker's wages kept the family fed and clothed.

3. A worker spent more time at the factory. This worker was viewed as a dedicated family man.

4. Women did not work in the factories. They only worked if they were unmarried, or at least childless.

5. Managers measured a worker's worth by time spent on the job. The reason managers did this was that they were responsible for production.

6. A worker took time off to tend to a sick family member. That worker was considered undependable.

7. Managers still measure worth in terms of hours. This happens despite the fact that the assembly line is no longer the model of American industry.

8. More women with children enter the workforce. This phenomenon has caused managers to reluctantly rethink their ideas about time and worth.

9. Human services professionals have studied work/family problems. These same human services professionals encourage corporations to become more flexible about time spent on the job.

10. At some point corporations will become more sensitive to the time constraints faced by workers. Meanwhile, both family and business will suffer.

Building Emphasis with Coordination and Subordination 113

EXERCISE 13-3: Revising for emphasis

Revise the following sentences by eliminating illogical or excessive coordination; inappropriate or ambiguous use of subordinating conjunctions; and illogical or excessive subordination.

EXAMPLE: By the age of four, Wolfgang Amadeus Mozart's musical ability was well known in Salzburg, and he became the court organist for the Archbishop.

REVISION: By the age of four, Wolfgang Amadeus Mozart's musical ability was well known in Salzburg, where he became the court organist for the Archbishop.

1. As his fame had spread before he was seven, he was invited to tour Europe in 1763.

2. Throughout his life, he composed in his head, where other composers agonized over the clavier.

3. By the time Mozart was fourteen, he had played for the crowned heads of Europe, and he played for the Pope also, and he had been writing sonatas for seven years at this time, and the Pope conferred on him the order of the Golden Spur, but Mozart did not think much of the award.

4. During his early years, Mozart performed in Germany, Austria, and Italy, and several heads of state commissioned sonatas and operas from him.

5. Mozart, like many composers before him, wrote music for religious occasions.

6. In 1777 the Archbishop, who knew that Mozart wished to move on, allowed the young man to take on other work, after which Mozart traveled to Paris and Munich, which were then centers of great music, because he wanted to expand his experience.

7. He spent a good deal of time in Vienna, as he wanted desperately to secure an appointment at the imperial court.

8. In late 1787 the Emperor finally hired Mozart and paid the young man less than half what his predecessor had been paid.

9. While employed by the Emperor, Mozart wrote operas and concertos, and he often performed himself, and some of his performances included improvisations, and the audience went wild over them.

10. Where he wrote in many forms, Mozart is most highly regarded for his operas.

Building Emphasis with Coordination and Subordination

EXERCISE 13-4: Combining sentences using subordination

Combine the following sentences using subordination.

EXAMPLE: Kandinsky was a Russian painter. Many consider him the founder of abstract art.

REVISION: Many consider the Russian painter Kandinsky the founder of abstract art.

1. The Walters Art Gallery was opened in 1931. It was founded by a father and son.

2. A U.S. passport is not required for travel to most countries in North, South, and Central America. A passport provides the best evidence of citizenship.

3. Many experts advise buying an inexpensive home in an expensive neighborhood. Its property value is likely to increase.

4. A bill is introduced by a senator or representative. The bill goes to the appropriate Senate or House committee.

5. Rachel Carson's book *Silent Spring* marks the beginning of the environmental movement. The book was published in 1962.

6. Transcendentalism was promoted by Emerson and Thoreau. It is a philosophy that holds that an ideal spiritual reality exists beyond the material world.

7. Genealogy is the study of family histories. Many Americans have become increasingly interested in genealogy.

8. A standard lease gives the landlord the right of reasonable access to the property. Usually, the landlord must provide at least 24 hours' notice before entering the property.

9. The Better Business Bureau is a nonprofit organization. One of its functions is to keep records of complaints about specific companies.

10. An eclipse usually lasts only a few minutes. The sun, moon, and Earth do not remain in alignment, but instead are in constant motion.

Building Emphasis with Coordination and Subordination 117

EXERCISE 13-5: Changing the emphasis in a sentence

Each sentence below contains a main clause and a subordinate clause. Rewrite each sentence so that the information in the subordinate clause appears in a main clause, and vice versa.

EXAMPLE: *Consumer Reports*, which accepts no advertising, often criticizes manufacturers and their products.

REVISION: *Consumer Reports*, which often criticizes manufacturers and their products, accepts no advertising.

1. Although tattooing is becoming increasingly popular, it is subject to very little regulation or quality control.

2. The philosophers called the cynics, so named because of their dog-like sneer, were founded by Diogenes.

3. The Islam religion, which has more than one billion followers, forbids the consumption of pork and alcohol.

4. After Shakespeare wrote his best comedies, he wrote his best tragedies.

5. Because I overslept, I was late for work.

6. Internal parasites in an animal, in addition to causing lethargy and poor appetite, make it vulnerable to infections.

7. While Scots celebrate Hogmaney Day on December 31, the Japanese celebrate Omisoka, meaning Grand Last Day.

8. Unlike Tennessee, which falls into two time zones, Virginia falls into only one.

9. Because many dot.com companies have failed to make a profit, thousands of their employees have been downsized.

10. A duke, whose wife is called a duchess, is of higher rank than an earl.

EXERCISE 13-6: Recognizing emphasis

Make three photocopies of several consecutive paragraphs from one of your textbooks. On the first copy, underline all coordinate structures, and identify the words indicating equal ideas as coordinating conjunctions, correlative conjunctions, or conjunctive adverbs. How many times does the writer use coordination? How often are works joined? phrases? clauses? How does the use of coordination help the writer achieve emphasis in the passage?

Building Emphasis with Coordination and Subordination

Using the second photocopy, underline all subordinate structures and circle each subordinating conjunction. What kind of relationships does each subordinating conjunction establish? (Refer to the list in the text.) How many times does the writer use subordination? How often are subordinate clauses placed at the beginning of the sentence? in the middle? at the end? How does the use of subordination help the writer achieve emphasis in the passage?

Using the third photocopy, underline and identify all special techniques for achieving emphasis. How many times does the writer use special techniques? How many different techniques does the author use? How does the use of special techniques help the writer achieve emphasis in the passage?

EXERCISE 13-7: Review

Rewrite the following paragraph, combining sentences with the techniques for achieving emphasis covered in this chapter.

    In the past twenty years, there has been a boom in medicine in this country. That boom has not been in human medicine. Dogs and cats who suffered illnesses were once "put to sleep." Now they are treated in much the same way as humans are. Some people consider pet health care a frivolous notion. Thousands of owners spend millions of dollars annually on treatment for their pets. Many owners consider their pets part of their family. These owners see nothing wrong with spending money for veterinary care. More people wish to treat rather than euthanize their pets. Pet health insurance programs are available around the country. Pet health care may be an indication of compassion. It may be an indication of misplaced priorities. It looks like many people will continue to pay the veterinarian to cure the family dog.

EXERCISE 13-8: Revising

As you revise drafts of any papers you're working on at present, use the techniques covered in this chapter to achieve emphasis. Remember that the ideas you want to communicate will determine the specific technique you use. Compare the revision to the original. How has adding emphasis improved the effectiveness of your paper?

CHAPTER 14

Choosing the Right Word

For use with Chapter 41 of *The Academic Writer's Handbook*

EXERCISE 14-1: Using a dictionary

Identify the dictionary that you use for this exercise. (If your instructor has assigned a particular dictionary, use that one.)

A. For each of the following words, first divide the word into syllables, then indicate its part of speech, and finally write out the current meaning listed in the dictionary. (Remember that the current meaning is not listed first in every dictionary.)

EXAMPLE	**Syllabification**	**Part of Speech**
magnanimous	mag nan i mous	adjective
noble, generous		

1. dispassionate _____ _____

2. solecism _____ _____

3. peripatetic _____ _____

4. tremulous _____ _____

5. hortatory _____ _____

6. vague _____ _____

7. evanescent _____ _____

Exercise Book for *The Academic Writer's Handbook*

8. quintessence _____ _____

9. zoomorphism _____ _____

10. bathos _____ _____

B. List all of the parts of speech that each of the following words can serve as.

EXAMPLE: market   noun, verb, adjective

1. contract _____

2. practice _____

3. degenerate _____

4. reserve _____

5. mirror _____

C. Write out all possible plural forms for the following nouns.

EXAMPLE: bench   benches

1. wharf _____

2. moose _____

3. attorney _____

4. radius _____

5. synthesis _____

Choosing the Right Word   123

D. Fill in the past, past participle, and present participle forms of the following verbs.

EXAMPLE	**Past**	**Past Part.**	**Pres. Part.**
think	thought	thought	thinking

1. swim _____   _____   _____

2. dream _____   _____   _____

3. cling _____   _____   _____

4. forget _____   _____   _____

5. hide _____   _____   _____

E. Fill in the comparative and superlative forms of the following adjectives and adverbs.

EXAMPLE	**Comparative**	**Superlative**
wonderful	more wonderful	most wonderful

1. possible _____   _____

2. quickly _____   _____

3. steep _____   _____

4. rapid _____   _____

5. final _____   _____

124   Exercise Book for *The Academic Writer's Handbook*

F.   Fill in the usage label assigned to each of the following words.

EXAMPLE
rumble (a fight)   slang

1. wicked (really)   _____

2. grinder (sandwich)   _____

3. thine   _____

4. post (courier)   _____

5. post (to mail)   _____

EXERCISE 14-2: Using a dictionary

Identify the dictionary that you use for this exercise. (If your instructor has assigned a particular dictionary, use that one.)

A.   Use an electronic or traditional thesaurus to find at least five synonyms and two antonyms for each word.

EXAMPLE: hide

SYNONYMS: conceal, cover, obscure, shroud, disguise

ANTONYMS: expose, display

1. clear (adj.)   _____

2. confirm   _____

3. doubt (verb)   _____

Choosing the Right Word   125

4. severe _____

5. teacher _____

6. radical (noun) _____

7. discipline _____

8. awesome _____

9. collection _____

10. develop _____

B. Use an electronic or traditional dictionary to check the pronunciation of each word. In particular, determine which syllable is stressed and what its vowel sound is. Do any words have divided pronunciations? If so, which pronunciation is listed first?

EXAMPLE: New Orleans: <u>noo áwrleenz</u>, <u>noo áwrlinz</u>, <u>noo awrléenz</u>

1. amenable _____

2. formidable _____

3. Goethe _____

4. either _____

5. leisure _____

6. often _____

7. pedagogy _____

8. prestigious _____

9. simultaneous _____

10. Thames _____

C. Look up the etymology of each of the following words in an electronic or traditional dictionary.

EXAMPLE: vermicelli: from Italian *vermicello* "'little worms"

1. acrobat _____

2. bit (computer term) _____

3. chauvinism _____

4. checkmate _____

5. fraction _____

6. limousine _____

7. Mardi Gras _____

8. mesmerize _____

9. philosophy _____

10. sarcasm _____

11. scuba _____

12. slogan _____

13. surgeon _____

14. tenure _____

EXERCISE 14-3: Analyzing the connotations of words

For each of the following words, identify two or three synonyms that have different connotations, and describe the connotation of each one.

EXAMPLE: group

ANSWER: club, gang, clique. *Club* carries no negative connotations, but suggests a group assembled for a recreational or social activity. *Gang* connotes a group assembled for illegal purposes. *Clique* connotes an elite, snobbish group that is closed to new members.

1. religious group

2. old person

3. young child

4. communicate

5. smart person

6. unconventional person

7. proud

8. old furniture

9. clever

10. relax

EXERCISE 14-4: Choosing words from the right register

Replace the underlined word or phrase in each sentence with one that is more suitable for academic writing.

EXAMPLE: The guy who runs the bookstore sets the buy-back prices for textbooks.

REVISION: The bookstore manager sets the buy-back prices for textbooks.

1. The health officer decided to check out the restaurant's kitchen.

2. Many people are really ticked off when they are put on hold.

3. It was <u>awesome</u> to finally be able to get all the courses I wanted.

4. You cannot <u>hassle</u> a suspect unless an attorney is present.

5. For a reader unfamiliar with computer jargon, it can be hard to <u>get a handle on</u> the author's point.

6. The most successful salespeople are willing to <u>go the whole nine yards</u> for their customers.

7. The television commentators <u>really went overboard</u> on their coverage of this event.

8. It was <u>a sure thing</u> that the incumbent would win the election.

9. The future of the company is <u>kind of shaky</u>.

10. The Sphinx presents Oedipus with a <u>weird</u> riddle.

EXERCISE 14-5: Choosing words from the right register

Replace the underlined word or phrase in each sentence with one that is more suitable for academic writing.

EXAMPLE: I totally spaced out about the meeting.

REVISION: I completely forgot about the meeting.

1. Trying to locate a government document can be a pain in the neck.

2. The accountant got his client into hot water by misinterpreting the IRS statute.

3. Vanessa is really into reggae music.

4. His new movie is good for a few yucks, but his last one was better.

5. The inspector was grossed out by the conditions at the nursing home.

6. After his third exam in one day, Armand went home and crashed.

7. Li promised to keep an eye on my apartment while I'm out of town.

8. The marketing team is <u>under the gun</u> to submit its proposal by Thursday at noon.

9. The library has <u>a bunch of stuff</u> on therapeutic riding programs.

10. Although Thompson recently <u>bad-mouthed</u> the economic reform program, he didn't offer a better solution to the problem.

EXERCISE 14-6: Choosing specific words

For each of the following words, identify at least three more specific words (i.e., types of the thing, if a noun, or action, if a verb). Try to identify an entire word rather than simply adding an adjective or adverb.

EXAMPLE: walk (verb)

ANSWER: amble, shuffle, stride

1. eating establishment (noun)

2. movie (noun)

3. house (noun)

4. jewelry (noun)

5. drink (noun)

6. talk (verb)

7. look at (verb)

8. rain (verb)

9. drink (verb)

10. eat (verb)

EXERCISE 14-7: Avoiding biased language

For items 1-6, identify a gender-neutral replacement for each word/phrase. For items 7-10, revise each sentence to avoid a masculine generic pronoun, using a different revision technique for each sentence.

EXAMPLE: mailman

REVISION: mail carrier

1. fireman

2. chairman

3. male nurse

4. garbage man

5. waitress

6. clergyman

7. Each student should bring his notes to the final exam.

8. A good manager asks for input from his employees.

9. A Social Security recipient may begin collecting his benefits one month after his 65th birthday.

10. At the end of the ceremony, the rabbi blesses his congregation.

EXERCISE 14-8: Avoiding biased language

The passages below are taken from college textbooks and academic books written about 30 to 50 years ago. Revise each passage so that it does not contain biased language. Try to use some different strategies for doing this as you move from one passage to the next.

EXAMPLE: An elementary school teacher should make sure that her students practice good hygiene to avoid head lice.

REVISION: An elementary school teacher should make sure that students practice good hygiene to avoid head lice.

1. To be able to throw a "curve" ball is the ambition of every young boy, while the tendency to "hook" or "slice" is a mental hazard for practically all golf players. What causes baseballs and golf balls to curve? . . . To study this problem, let each of us picture himself as a baseball pitcher pitching the ball so that it spins counterclockwise when viewed from the top. (Source: L. Paul Elliott and William F. Wilcox, *Physics: A Modern Approach*. New York: Macmillan, 1959, p. 101.)

_____
_____
_____
_____
_____

2. A scientist, confronted with an individual thing, or a material, or a process in which he was interested, looked at it, if he were an Aristotelian, in terms derived from the metaphysics we have just sketched. (Source: R. Harr—, *The Philosophies of Science: An Introductory Survey*. London: Oxford University Press, 1972, p. 126.)

3. Even in a primitive economy men learn that, rather than have everyone do everything in a mediocre way, it is better to start a *division of labor*—better for fat men to do the fishing, lean men the hunting, and smart men to make the medicine, each exchanging his goods for the goods he needs. (Source: Paul A. Samuelson, *Economics: An Introductory Analysis*, 7th edition. New York: McGraw-Hill, 1967, pp. 50-51.)

4. Barter represents a great improvement over a state of affairs in which every man had to be a Jack-of-all-trades and master of none. A great debt of gratitude is owed to the first two ape men who suddenly perceived that each could be made better off by giving up some of one good in exchange for some of another. . . . In all but the most primitive cultures men do not directly exchange one good for another. (Source: Paul A. Samuelson, *Economics: An Introductory Analysis*, 7th edition. New York: McGraw-Hill, 1967, p. 52.)

5. We still feel that a student reads his textbook in his room, without an instructor on hand to translate it for him. So our major objective was to provide him with a book from which he could—by himself—gain a true picture of what calculus is all about. (Source: Robert C. Fisher and Allen D. Ziebur, *Calculus and Analytic Geometry*, 2nd edition. Englewood Cliffs, NJ: Prentice-Hall, 1965, p. v.)

EXERCISE 14-9: Building vocabulary

Locate in one of your textbooks a passage that includes several words that are new to you. Before looking them up in the dictionary, try to determine their meaning based on the context. Write out your tentative definition, and then check it with the dictionary definition. If the meanings are close, you've done a good job of making an educated guess.

CHAPTER 15

Using End Punctuation

For use with Chapter 42 of *The Academic Writer's Handbook*

EXERCISE 15-1: Using the period

Add, delete, or move periods as needed in the following sentences, paying particular attention to quotation marks and parentheses.

EXAMPLE: The United Nations was born in San Francisco in 1945

REVISION: The United Nations was born in San Francisco in 1945.

1. The end of World War II. brought many changes to the balance of power in the world

2. Much of Eastern Europe came under Soviet control (Tito, however, successfully retained Yugoslavia's sovereignty).

3. The Allies formed the North Atlantic Treaty Organization to protect western Europe from aggression

4. N.A.T.O. became known as "the protector of European democracy".

5. France and England eventually gave up many of their colonies The battle over Algerian independence from France was finally settled by Gen Charles De Gaulle.

6. The U.N. intervened in the civil war in Korea in 1950 (between the Soviet-supported North and the U. S.-supported South.).

7. The superpowers which emerged at the end of W. W. II were the United States and the Union of Soviet Socialist Republics, or U. S. S. R.

8. The Soviet Union's Nikita Khrushchev threatened the US, "We will bury you.".

9. Mr Khrushchev did more to instill fear of Communism in American school children than did Stalin, according to Catherine Mahoney, PhD..

10. President Eisenhower swore that "Communism will never prevail.", comforting children across the country.

EXERCISE 15-2: Using the question mark

Add, delete, or move question marks as needed in the following sentences, paying particular attention to quotation marks.

EXAMPLE: The question to be considered is, do children lie in court testimony.

REVISION: The question to be considered is, do children lie in court testimony?

1. Did you hear the judge ask, "Are you sure this is what happened?"?

2. The defense attorney asked why the child had changed his testimony?

3. Were the prosecutors and the child's father "playing games?"

4. The defense called in an expert (?) to support the mother's testimony.

5. Could the child have been prompted, convinced that his story was true, perhaps even provided with the story.

6. Experts disagree on whether or not children lie in court?

7. A figure of 2 percent (?) is usually cited as the percentage of children who lie in court.

8. Some researchers are asking if that percentage is valid?

9. Which studies should we believe.

10. "How can we ever know?", asked one psychologist.

EXERCISE 15-3: Using exclamation points

Add, delete, or move exclamation points as needed in the following sentences.

EXAMPLE: When the year 2000 was about to arrive, some people believed that the end of the world was at hand!

REVISION: When the year 2000 was about to arrive, some people believed that the end of the world was at hand.

1. As I started to sit down, my husband shouted, "Wait. There's a cat on your chair."

2. As we crossed the crowded street, another pedestrian suddenly yelled, "Look out!".

3. "The bus driver just had a heart attack!," shouted one of the passengers in the front row.

4. Even young children can experience the signs of stress! These include muscle tension, nausea, and headaches.

5. "The Gulf War signaled the beginning of Armageddon"! cried one believer.

EXERCISE 15-4: Review

Provide periods, question marks, and exclamation points as needed in the following paragraph.

David Attenborough has spent his life asking questions. And what a life He is a noted scientist, a respected author, and a successful producer for television Mr Attenborough criticizes theories that explain the purpose of human life in purely biological terms If human beings exist solely to carry on the species, he asks, then how do you explain the arts philanthropy educational reform Attenborough explains these phenomena as "externalized inheritance" It doesn't take a PhD, he says, to see that society contributes as much to an individual's development as does genetics An individual's development is shaped not only by personal heredity, but by the Rockefeller Foundation, humanist philosophy, and UNICEF, among other things According to one student of Attenborough's, "This man believes in limitless possibilities for the human race"

CHAPTER 16

Using Commas

For use with Chapter 43 of *The Academic Writer's Handbook*

EXERCISE 16-1: Using commas with introductory and concluding expressions

In the following sentences, insert commas to set off introductory elements and interrupting elements. Circle the number of any sentences in which no comma is needed.

EXAMPLE: The medical technology boom that began in the late 19th century according to scientific historians resulted in the abandonment of many home remedies.

REVISION: The medical technology boom that began in the late 19th century, **according to scientific historians**, resulted in the abandonment of many home remedies.

1. Before the boom people used herbs and natural concoctions to treat injuries and illness.

2. For example camphor was often used to ease headache pain.

3. Honey not cough medicine was used to relieve nagging coughs.

4. People have been returning to natural remedies in the past few years.

5. In addition they have been taking advantage of unfamiliar medical treatment especially acupuncture.

6. In acupuncture thin needles are placed just under the skin.

7. Alternative medical treatment regardless of its growing popularity is viewed with skepticism by traditionally educated doctors.

8. That skepticism is understandable of course.

9. In the first place natural remedies and alternative medicines do not operate on the same principles as traditional medicine.

10. Perhaps even more important such remedies compete with traditional medicine for business and respect.

EXERCISE 16-2: Using a comma and a coordinating conjunction between independent clauses

Combine the following sentences to form sentences in which two independent clauses are joined by a coordinating conjunction. Add commas or semicolons as needed.

EXAMPLE: Some developers are beginning to rethink the American suburb. They are looking to old-fashioned small towns for their inspiration.

REVISION: Some developers are beginning to rethink the American suburb, **and** they are looking to old-fashioned small towns for their inspiration.

1. One of the characteristics of the contemporary suburb is that residents have to drive everywhere. A new generation of planners is changing all that.

2. Because most housing developments have been built to accommodate vehicular traffic, pedestrian needs are often unmet. That emphasis on traffic has contributed to the isolation of the suburbs.

3. Planners Andres Duany and Elizabeth Plater-Zyberk design towns with old-fashioned town centers. The towns are completely up-to-date.

4. The emphasis in the towns designed by Duany and Plater-Zyberk is on community rather than on accessibility to highways. They don't worry about laying out streets that all feed into the nearest freeway entrance.

5. People living in such communities do not have to drive to a convenience store. They do not feel that the streets belong to cars rather than people.

EXERCISE 16-3: Using commas between items in a series

Add commas as necessary to the following sentences, placing optional commas in parentheses. If no commas are necessary, be prepared to explain why.

EXAMPLE: Among the many social problems in the United States are inadequate health care malnutrition and illiteracy among the poor.

REVISION: Among the many social problems in the United States are inadequate **health care, malnutrition(,) and illiteracy** among the poor.

1. One of the problems most difficult to solve is chronic widespread homelessness.

2. Homelessness has grown in the past several decades as a result of high housing costs severe drug problems and release of patients from state institutions.
3. Homelessness has emerged as a severe complex problem in American cities.
4. Many of the homeless simply need jobs medical care and housing.
5. Others need treatment for drug and alcohol addiction.
6. Still others cannot survive outside a protective controlled institution.
7. Many of the old reliable solutions don't seem to work.
8. Homeless people include families addicts and emotionally disturbed people.
9. The complexity of the problem makes it difficult to define analyze and solve.
10. A nation with such wealth education and technological skill should be able to solve the problem.

EXERCISE 16-4: Comma use with essential and nonessential elements

In the following sentences, determine whether or not the underlined phrases and clauses are essential or nonessential. Use commas accordingly.

EXAMPLE: Many writers <u>who chronicle the African-American experience</u> have been recognized in the United States for decades.

ANSWER: Essential—No commas needed.

1. Langston Hughes <u>whose poetry expresses the frustrations of racial injustice</u> is studied in literature programs across the country.

2. Zora Neale Hurston <u>a contemporary of Hughes's</u> provided inspiration for Alice Walker.

3. Within the past few years, African-American art <u>which had not received much attention previously</u> has been discovered by critics.

4. One of the more respected artists is Romare Bearden <u>a collagist</u>.

5. The work <u>that Bearden produced in the thirty years before his death in 1988</u> revolutionized the art of collage.

6. Bearden founded Spiral <u>a black artists' group</u> in the 1960s.

7. Much of the work <u>produced by members of the group</u> was motivated by the civil rights movement.

8. During the 1970s, Bearden <u>whose own work moved from abstract painting to collage</u> finally received the recognition he deserved.

9. Bearden's use of color was strongly influenced by the tropics <u>which contrasted with urban environments such as New York City</u>.

10. Bearden's work <u>which has toured the country</u> includes both urban and rural images.

EXERCISE 16-5: Using commas according to convention and to clarify meaning

Insert commas as needed in the following sentences.

EXAMPLE: The lecturer asked the audience "Who was the most influential person of all time?"

REVISION: The lecturer asked the audience, "Who was the most influential person of all time?"

A. Quotations, direct address, and tag questions

1. "I'd say it was either Mohammed, Jesus, or Confucius wouldn't you?"

2. "Couldn't it be" suggested the lecturer "someone more contemporary?"

3. "I think it was Karl Marx" offered one member of the audience.

4. "But his influence is already waning isn't it?"

5. "Members of the audience please make up your minds."

B. Balanced sentences, "more/less" constructions, and yes/no remarks

1. Half the audience believed that Marx was overrated; the other half that he deserved his position in history.

Using Commas 151

2. "No I wouldn't consider Marx one of the most influential people in history."

3. One person considered Plato the most influential person; another Aristotle.

4. The more the audience discussed the matter the less they agreed with each other.

5. "Oh well it isn't essential that we all agree."

C. Names, titles, dates, numbers, addresses; clarifying meaning

1. The lecturer was Kristin M. McArthur Ph.D.

2. She spoke before an audience of 1340 people.

3. By eight 500 people were waiting at the doors.

4. The lecture was telecast on Friday August 23 1991.

5. Requests for transcripts should be address to Tara Fitzgerald Vice President for Operations Northeast Speakers' Bureau 147 Atlantic Avenue Salem New Hampshire 03079.

EXERCISE 16-6: Eliminating misuse of commas

In the following sentences, remove inappropriate commas. Circle the number of any sentences in which commas are used appropriately.

EXAMPLE: The Sandinista Revolution, overthrew the Somoza government in Nicaragua in 1979.

REVISION: The Sandinista Revolution overthrew the Somoza government in Nicaragua in 1979.

1. The international community first became aware of the corruption in the Somoza regime after the 1972 earthquake, relief funds were diverted to the private use of Somoza and his cronies.

2. The assassination of newspaper editor, Pedro Chamorro, in 1978 provided added impetus to revolutionary forces.

3. The Somoza government left Nicaragua in economic, and social ruin.

4. Initially the revolutionary government, led by the Sandinistas, was immensely popular.

5. Dissatisfaction began as the government had trouble keeping, the promises it had made.

Using Commas 153

6. Resistance to Daniel Ortega's government was organized by the CIA, and right-wing forces in Nicaragua.

7. Elections were held in Nicaragua a little over a decade after the Sandinistas took power, the world was startled when Ortega lost.

8. The new President was Violetta Chamorro, widow of Pedro Chamorro.

9. Chamorro's coalition government, faced severe economic and political problems.

10. The inflation, that had plagued the Sandinistas, continued after Chamorro took office.

CHAPTER 17

Using Semicolons

For use with Chapter 44 of *The Academic Writer's Handbook*

EXERCISE 17-1: Using a semicolon to join independent clauses

Combine the following sentences, using semicolons (with or without conjunctive adverbs) to join independent clauses.

EXAMPLE: In 1972, Dartmouth College hired an anthropology instructor to head a new program in Native-American studies. The man's name was Michael Dorris.

REVISION: In 1972, Dartmouth College hired an anthropology instructor to head a new program in Native-American studies; the man's name was Michael Dorris.

1. Dorris had lived for a time on an Indian reservation. Most of his early years were spent in Louisville, Kentucky.

2. As a single man, Dorris adopted three children. He provided them with a family atmosphere.

3. One of his children had trouble learning. Dorris took him to many doctors.

4. The doctors in New Hampshire could not diagnose his son's problem. The director of an Indian program on a South Dakota reservation recognized fetal alcohol syndrome.

5. Dorris's book about his son, *The Broken Cord*, sold over 75,000 copies. The story has touched people across the country.

6. Dorris and his future wife, writer Louise Erdrich, met at Dartmouth in the mid-1970s. They had three children together.

7. Erdrich was also a writer. Her first novel, *Love Medicine*, won the National Book Critics Circle Award for 1984.

8. Dorris and Erdrich regularly edited and criticized each other's work. In 1988, they actually began writing a novel together.

9. *The Crown of Columbus* was a reflection on the 500th anniversary of Columbus's discovery of America. It explored the discovery from the perspective of the native people.

10. During the 1990s, Dorris's life was beset by legal and personal difficulties. Dorris took his own life on April 11, 1997.

EXERCISE 17-2: Using a semicolon to prevent misreading

Insert semicolons as needed in the following sentences to prevent misreading.

EXAMPLE: The Parker River National Wildlife Refuge, which provides nesting areas for the endangered piping plover, is sometimes closed to human traffic, but many people who use the area for recreation feel that the service is not responsive to their concerns.

REVISION: The Parker River National Wildlife Refuge, which provides nesting areas for the endangered piping plover, is sometimes closed to human traffic; but many people who use the area for recreation feel that the service is not responsive to their concerns.

1. The refuge is used by hikers, who find the beach trails peaceful, by sports enthusiasts, who consider the ocean and river fishing incomparable, and by sunbathers, who recognize the beach at the refuge as one of the finest in New England.

2. Closing the beach is clearly an unpopular decision, according to the manager of the refuge, and area residents who depend on the beach for recreational activities have reason to be angry.

3. The manager emphasizes that the business of the Fish and Wildlife Service is to protect animals, not to provide recreation for humans, but privately he acknowledges that decisions to close popular areas are difficult not only for vacationers, but for the local economy as well.

4. Among the threats to piping plovers are beachgoers, who often trample newborn chicks, animal predators, which are attracted by human garbage, and pollution, which destroys the plovers' food.

5. Soon after they hatch, plover chicks can walk on their own, but they cannot fly for at least a month, making it difficult for them to evade the human onslaught on sunny summer days.

EXERCISE 17-3: Correct use of semicolons

Correct any problems in the use of the semicolon in the following sentences.

EXAMPLE: The senator assured the students that they would get help with their financial aid, nevertheless, many of them remain concerned about their tuition.

REVISION: The senator assured the students that they would get help with their financial aid; nevertheless, many of them remain concerned about their tuition.

1. Linguists insist that no human language is "primitive"; even if it does not exist in a written form.

2. Use one of the following graphics formats; JPEG, GIF, or Bitmap.

3. The participants at the conference included; Meg Ashton, Director of Development, Ben Suarez, Director of Personnel, and Syd Coleman, Director of Community Relations.

4. The air temperature is 5° F, the wind chill is –20° F.

5. Many players try to cheat in Las Vegas, as a result, elaborate security measures are in place in the casinos.

6. The state motto of Nebraska is "Equality before the law;" that of Wyoming is "Equal Rights."

7. When the new tax law goes into effect next month; many small businesses will be eligible for its benefits.

8. Because it is essentially property; a patent may be sold or assigned to someone other than the original inventor.

9. I waited 30 minutes for the bus; but it never came.

10. The realtor showed us three houses on Sunday, however, none of them had all the features that we want.

EXERCISE 17-4: Correct use of semicolons

Correct any problems in the use of the semicolon in the following sentences.

EXAMPLE:	Although eco-labels are appearing on more and more products; their use is not governed by consistent guidelines.
REVISION:	Although eco-labels are appearing on more and more products, their use is not governed by consistent guidelines.

1. A recent study showed that British women who drank at least one cup of tea per day; had denser bones than those who didn't.

Using Semicolons   161

2. Some Supreme Court justices; especially Antonin Scalia and Clarence Thomas, tend to vote more conservatively than others.

3. Until the success of the Harry Potter books; it was unusual for boys to be attracted to books by female authors.

4. In 1981, 11,500 air traffic controllers went on strike, they were fired by President Reagan.

5. Examples of herbal theme gardens include Shakespeare gardens, with bay, calendula, lemon balm, and rue, Biblical gardens, with costmary, hyssop, mandrake, saffron, and sesame, and bee gardens, with bee balm, comfrey, mint, and pennyroyal.

6. Some people swear by newspaper for cleaning windows, however, others hate it.

7. The Pilgrims were not as dull as we may think, for example, they frequently drank beer.

8. Several drivers have won the Indianapolis 500 more than once; including Wilbur Shaw, Bill Vukovich, A. J. Foyt, Al Unser, and Rick Mears.

9. Traditionally, the bride's family paid most wedding expenses, today, both families are likely to share the expenses.

10. Two of my favorite authors, John Cheever and John Updike; set much of their work in the suburbs.

EXERCISE 17-5: Revising

Now that you have a good understanding of the various uses of the comma and the semicolon, apply that knowledge when revising your papers. Reread the drafts of any papers you're working on at present, and decide where commas and semicolons might be appropriate. Check also for instances where you may have misused or overused commas and semicolons.

CHAPTER 18

Using Apostrophes

For use with Chapter 45 of *The Academic Writer's Handbook*

EXERCISE 18-1: Possessive forms

Fill in the appropriate possessive form for each of the following nouns, using apostrophes when necessary.

EXAMPLE: women   women's

1. actress

2. it

3. master of ceremonies

4. Melissa and Jason (jointly)

5. The Blakes

6. her

7. Shannon and Jim (individually)

8. sergeant-at-arms

9. children

10. movie

EXERCISE 18-2: Distinguishing between possessives and contractions, plural nouns, and singular verbs

In the following sentences, underline the appropriate form of each word in parentheses.

EXAMPLE: If (your/<u>you're</u>) trying to lose weight, beware of the quick and painless programs.

1. (Doctors/Doctor's) agree that the only way to lose weight and keep it off is to change (your/you're) eating habits.

2. Most people who use a commercial diet program regain (their/they're) weight within two years.

3. If you use a commercial program, you should understand that the (programs/program's) interests sometimes lie more in the profits (their/they're) going to make than in (your/you're) well-being.

4. If the program (guarantees/guarantee's) that you will lose weight, (your/you're) probably going to be disappointed.

5. A program that places good nutrition at (its/it's) center is the best choice.

EXERCISE 18-3: Using apostrophes in contractions and plural forms

A. Combine the following words to form contractions.

EXAMPLE: would + not   wouldn't

1. could + have   _____

2. they + will   _____

3. we + are   _____

4. you + had   _____

5. have + not   _____

6. she + is   _____

7. she + has   _____

8. will + not   _____

9. we + will   _____

10. they + are   _____

B. Form the plurals of the following letters, words, and numbers.

1. 7   _____

2. r   _____

3. #   _____

4. trust (referred to as a word)   _____

5. D   _____

EXERCISE 18-4: Reviewing use of apostrophes

Add or remove apostrophes as needed in the following sentences.

EXAMPLE: How many As did Tomas make last semester?

REVISION: How many A's did Tomas make last semester?

1. Its never too late to improve your study habits.

2. Reagan and Clinton's administrations both lasted eight years.

3. Mens clothing is located in the back of the store.

4. While HMO's are often criticized, our local one works quite well.

5. A clich— is an overused expression, like "You can't judge a book by it's cover."

6. As the 90's came to a close, business' waited anxiously for potential Y2K problems to emerge.

7. Tom Hanks movies are known for their high quality and box-office success.

Using Apostrophes 167

8. In a backlash against dot.com's, one furniture companys billboard features big red Xs through the "www" and ".com" of it's Web address.

9. Geoffreys Achilles heel is his ego.

10. My aunt consider's herself an accomplished pianist.

EXERCISE 18-5: Reviewing use of apostrophes

Add or remove apostrophes as needed in the following sentences.

EXAMPLE: The two Tappet Brother's show, "Car Talk," is on NPR.

REVISION: The two Tappet Brothers' show, "Car Talk," is on NPR.

1. Paula and Chris' GPAs are identical.

2. The Smith's are going to Florida on their vacation.

3. Many cereal manufacturer's are expanding into snack foods.

4. That store is having it's fifth "Going out of Business" sale.

5. The Wilsons contributions to the arts have been honored with a commemorative plaque.

6. Several different family's owned this house during the 1990's.

7. Are tomato's a vegetable or a fruit?

8. Womens' colleges are not as common as they once were.

9. The National Weather Services long-range forecast say's it's going to be the coldest winter in several years.

10. Her last two CD's have been very derivative.

EXERCISE 18-6: Reviewing use of apostrophes

Insert or delete apostrophes as needed in the following paragraph.

PBS's series *I, Claudius* is based on Robert Graves book. Various historians accounts of the period are used by Graves, who begins his tale with reference to Antony's and Cleopatra's defeat. Chronicling the Roman emperors from Augustus to Claudius, the series focus's on the corruption and treachery that eventually led to the fall of Rome. Of all the villains in the series, Claudius grandmother Livia is perhaps the worst. In order to insure that her son Tiberius will become emperor, Livia either poisons or otherwise arranges the death's of various members of her family, including her husband. (Its even suggested that she poisons her own son.) The emperor of Romes position at the time was all powerful; Rome ruled much of the world, and the emperor almost single-handedly ruled Rome. Livias activities are designed to help history on it's way. Claudius comes to suspect her treachery, but few people take him seriously because hes a cripple and he stutter's. His stammering buh-buh-buhs annoy the family, but they also protect him—nobody believes that Claudius is smart enough to be dangerous. The result is that Claudius outlives his ill-fated family. The history that he writes at the end of his life is their's.

CHAPTER 19

Using Quotation Marks

For use with Chapter 46 of *The Academic Writer's Handbook*

EXERCISE 19-1: Quoting prose

Rewrite the following sentences, using the appropriate marks to indicate quotations, and making sure that the quotation marks and other marks are placed appropriately. Words to be quoted are underlined; double underlining indicates quoted material within quotations.

EXAMPLE: In *Children of War*, Roger Rosenblatt describes Cambodian refugee children as <u>astonishingly beautiful</u>.

REVISION: In *Children of War*, Roger Rosenblatt describes Cambodian refugee children as "astonishingly beautiful."

1. Ty Kim Seng is a boy <u>who was forced to join one of the mobile work teams instituted by Pol Pot for the Khmer children's education and well-being</u>, according to Rosenblatt.

2. In talking to children of war-torn countries, Rosenblatt discovers that he has being <u>defining vengeance conventionally</u>; one child he speaks to says, <u>To me, revenge means that I must make the most of my life</u> (471).

3. Rosenblatt asks himself, <u>Could their idea of revenge thus be a way of dealing with the fear of evil in themselves</u>?

4. Rosenblatt keeps hearing the same refrain—<u>revenge is to make a bad man better than before</u>—in his talks with the children.

5. Is it any wonder that these children believe that <u>peace is worth more than gold</u>?

EXERCISE 19-2: Quoting dialogue

Rewrite the following dialogue, supplying the appropriate paragraphing, quotation marks, and other punctuation.

EXAMPLE: Have you ever heard, asked Joanne, of Max Ernst?

REVISION: "Have you ever heard," asked Joanne, "of Max Ernst?"

I replied, no, tell me about him. Joanne thought for a moment: well, she said, he created bizarre images—collages, really—that juxtaposed beasts, plants, and humans. When did he do his work, I asked. Joanne replied, He painted from 1920 until well into the '50s, but his best work was done before 1940. I asked where I could see his work displayed. Most of it is in European galleries, Joanne reluctantly admitted.

EXERCISE 19-3: Reviewing use of quotation marks

Correct any errors in the use of quotation marks in the following sentences.

EXAMPLE: "Harry Potter and the Sorcerer's Stone" was a bestseller among children and adults alike.

REVISION: *Harry Potter and the Sorcerer's Stone* was a bestseller among children and adults alike.

1. Some critics call "On Golden Pond" Henry Fonda's best movie.

2. The definition of fair use of copyrighted material varies according to the type of material.

3. "Man was born free" said Rousseau "and everywhere he is in chains".

4. The researchers warned the company "that they would not be responsible for any injuries caused by the experiment."

5. In what one observer called a 'breathtaking' turn of events, the Supreme Court reversed the lower court's decision.

6. John Belushi achieved a kind of entertainment "Triple Crown:" successes in music, the movies, and television.

7. In what work does Descartes say "I think, therefore I am?"

8. According to Jane Bryant Quinn: "Pawnshops and shops giving "loans until payday" are sprouting in the suburbs."

9. Jesse Ventura's book "Do I Stand Alone?" includes a chapter called What's Keeping the American Political System from Working as Well as It Should?

10. Sungsume announced "I refuse to participate in the debate".

Using Quotation Marks 175

EXERCISE 19-4: Reviewing use of quotation marks

Correct any errors in the use of quotation marks in the following sentences.

EXAMPLE: Sylvia Plath's only novel, "The Bell Jar," is drawn from her own experiences.

REVISION: Sylvia Plath's only novel, *The Bell Jar,* is drawn from her own experiences.

1. Mannitol is used as the dust on chewing gum.

2. The author's third chapter, The Language of Poems, defines a number of common literary terms.

3. According to an article about a new treatment for warts, "76 percent of the patients were "very happy" with the results."

4. The city council members called for "an end to partisan politics", but unfortunately their actions have not contributed to this goal.

5. With respect to wine, room temperature can be defined as 65 to 68 degrees Fahrenheit.

6. Mariel announced that "she was going to win the scholarship."

7. According to one critic, Cheever reaches the pinnacle of his talent in short stories like "The Country Husband".

8. A recent article states that, to attract home-schooled children to public schools, some school districts "are getting entrepreneurial;" they offer weekly classes in everything from computer skills to modern dance.

9. According to "Newsweek," the theme song for the Bush-Gore campaign was "Who Let the Dogs Out"?

10. One source confirmed that, "A shortage of flu vaccine may lead to increased business losses due to employee absenteeism".

EXERCISE 19-5: Reviewing use of quotation marks

Insert, move, or delete quotation marks as needed in the following paragraph.

    I was reminded the other day of a statement from Margaret Mead's book *Male and Female:* "Every home is different from every other home. (76)" As I think back over my childhood, I realize how right she was. In our home, we answered not only to my mother and father, but to my grandmother and Pop-Pop as well. My best friend "Cindy," however, found our large family strange: Why are there so many people in your house—and so many bosses? she would ask. I, on the other hand, could not understand the rigid "sex roles" in her family. I could never visit her house without thinking of the children's story Dick and Jane Play Grownup. The story had always seemed so strange to me, with its clear distinctions between men's work and women's work. And again, as I think back on that time, I remember Margaret Mead's words. I once heard her tell a story about what she called the greatest threat to sex roles in the American family: taking out the garbage. Mead was talking about the fact that traditional sex roles call for males to be responsible only for outside work and women for inside work. Since garbage originates inside the home, she explained, smiling benignly, but ends up outside, whose job is it to take out the garbage? I appreciate that story now as my husband and I take turns with the garbage, and I think of how different the family we have built is from either his family or mine. I find it "remarkable" that what Mead wrote and talked about years ago remains true today.

CHAPTER 20

Using Other Marks

For use with Chapter 47 of *The Academic Writer's Handbook*

EXERCISE 20-1: Using the colon

In the following sentences, insert and delete colons where necessary. Circle the number of any correct sentences.

EXAMPLE: In the 1950s, some liberal-leaning parents feared three things, Senator Joseph McCarthy, the crusading newspapers, and their children.

REVISION: In the 1950s, some liberal-leaning parents feared three things: Senator Joseph McCarthy, the crusading newspapers, and their children.

1. Many refused to take seriously the specter of child-informants: in fact, they scoffed at the idea.

2. Some, however, related stories of: radio commentators urging children to inform on parents and teachers quizzing students about their parents' politics.

3. Regardless of the legitimacy of these fears, one thing was abundantly clear: McCarthy's campaign was tearing some families apart.

4. Some observers see a similar situation with today's children: except that today, children are criticizing their parents for ecological reasons.

5. One eight-year-old wrote a formal letter to her mother. "Dear Mom, Stop running the water when you brush your teeth. Love, Leanne."

6. Kids by the thousands have brought ecology handbooks such as the EarthWorks Group's *Fifty Simple Things Kids Can Do to Save the Earth* (Kansas City, Andrews McNeel, 1990) and Gail Gibbons' *Recycle, A Handbook for Kids* (Boston, Little Brown & Co., 1996).

7. Today's children express concern about pollution, depletion of the ozone layer, animal rights, and human health; they're a generation of eco-activists.

8. Many parents who came of age in the '60s see their children as crusaders for a better world.

9. They like what they see, a generation committed to a better world.

10. One parent put it this way, "If my kids pester me about saving energy, then I know I've done a good job bringing them up."

EXERCISE 20-2: Using the dash

In the following sentences, insert dashes where appropriate for emphasis.

EXAMPLE: Recently a forgotten group of Holocaust survivors hidden children began to speak up.

REVISION: Recently a forgotten group of Holocaust survivors—hidden children—began to speak up.

1. These children spent the World War II years in hiding, an experience that was sometimes as frightening as being in the concentration camps.

2. One survivor describes her situation huddled in a basement with a dozen other frightened children as one in which the fear of being caught plagued everyone constantly.

3. These hidden children have often been told that they were lucky, they survived.

4. Explaining why she has finally begun to speak of her experience, Nicole David says, "If we don't tell our story it will be forgotten, or falsified or denied."

5. Separation from parents, denial of heritage, fear of discovery, these were the daily concerns of hidden children.

EXERCISE 20-3: Using parentheses

Add, change, or remove parentheses where appropriate in the following sentences, altering placement of punctuation as necessary.

EXAMPLE: The Food and Drug Administration FDA investigates misleading labels on prepared foods.

REVISION: The Food and Drug Administration (FDA) investigates misleading labels on prepared foods.

1. According to one critic, "Beethoven's Pastural (sic) Symphony is his greatest work."

2. The vocal ensemble specializes in music performed without accompaniment (also known as *a cappella* music (literally "in the church style")).

3. The most common signs of shock include the following: 1, a weak, rapid pulse, 2, "cold sweat," 3, faintness and weakness, and 4, anxious behavior.

4. Malcolm X, (born Malcolm Little in 1925), who changed his name after adopting the Islamic religion, was assassinated in 1965.

5. The principle of Ockham's razor (attributed to William of Ockham (1285-1349)) states that the simpler of two competing theories should be preferred.

EXERCISE 20-4: Using brackets, ellipses, and the slash

Follow the instructions for each item, using brackets, ellipses, and the slash as appropriate.

EXAMPLE: Delete the second verb: "Most people do not remember or appreciate Zachary Taylor's contributions to the American presidency."

REVISION: "Most people do not remember . . . Zachary Taylor's contributions to the American presidency."

1. Add the clarification "Old Rough and Ready" to indicate the nickname: "Those who gave Taylor his nickname would be amazed at his obscurity."

2. Rewrite the fraction in digits: Taylor died after serving only a little more than one quarter of his term.

3. Delete the final phrase: "Historians had agreed that Taylor died from food poisoning, until novelist Clara Rising suggested that he may have been poisoned by political enemies."

4. <u>Acknowledge the misspelling</u>: "Tailor is now more famous than he had ever been in the past."

5. <u>Indicate a pause at the end of the first sentence</u>: Suppose we discover that Taylor really was poisoned. What do we do then?

EXERCISE 20-5: Review

Add colons, dashes, parentheses, brackets, ellipses, and slashes as needed in the following paragraph.

Red Adair The Forgotten John Wayne Hero

War heroes, renegades from the Old West, sturdy pioneers, these are the characters portrayed on the big screen by John Wayne. Not many ordinary citizens have been immortalized by the Duke. One relatively obscure person who can make such a claim is Red Adair his adventures were the subject of a 1969 movie called *The Hellfighters*. Adair was not a war hero or a pioneer, and he wasn't a notorious renegade from the Old West. So why does he have the honor of having been played by the Duke? It's Adair's business that made him so appealing to Hollywood. *Hellfighters* refers to those men and women in Adair's prime, mostly men who fight fires in oil wells. Unlike ordinary fires, oil fires are fed constantly by the fuel in the wells. And they're powerful so powerful that only a select few companies can take on the task of extinguishing an oil-well fire. Adair is a combination cowboy daredevil technician whose successes in putting out fires in Texas and Oklahoma inspired the Wayne movie. One of the hellfighters who works for Adair describes his boss in these terms "Red is Red is Well, Red is like no other man I've ever met. He looks just like a regular guy. But he can take on a well that's pumping flames 5,000 pounds of pressure." Such testimony is one of the reasons that Adair's company was called in to douse the oil fires left in Kuwait after the Gulf War "We wanted the best, and *Adair is better than the best* italics mine," said one Kuwaiti official.

CHAPTER 21

Using Capitals

For use with Chapter 48 of *The Academic Writer's Handbook*

EXERCISE 21-1: Using capitals

In the following sentences, add or delete capitals as necessary. Circle the number of any correct sentences.

EXAMPLE: On november 22, 1963, John F. Kennedy was assassinated.

REVISION: On November 22, 1963, John F. Kennedy was assassinated.

1. Kennedy was the fourth president to be assassinated. (the other three were Lincoln, Garfield, and McKinley.)

2. When Kennedy announced plans to go to dallas, democrats were concerned about his reception in the south.

3. Governor Connally of Texas met the president's plane, and the Governor assured Kennedy that texans would welcome him.

4. The general population was indeed receptive, except for a man perched in a window of the texas school book depository.

5. A former marine with a russian wife was arrested, spawning rumors of a communist conspiracy.
6. Before Lee Harvey Oswald could be tried, Businessman Jack Ruby shot him.
7. Since then, questions about conspiracy have continued to haunt the country: did Oswald act alone? was he part of a conspiracy? if so, who was behind the assassination? was cuba involved? did the mafia have Kennedy killed?
8. From north to south, east to west, the rumors flew.
9. The warren commission report concluded that Oswald acted alone, but new orleans district attorney Jim Garrison investigated and found conspiracy.
10. Since the Sixties, various theories about the Kennedy Assassination have been suggested, but to this day nobody can be sure of what really happened that day at dealey plaza.

EXERCISE 21-2: Using capitals

In the following sentences, add or delete capitals as necessary.

EXAMPLE: Most High School students take courses in english and mathematics during their Senior year.

REVISION: Most high school students take courses in English and mathematics during their senior year.

1. To get to Carnegie hall, turn North at central park.

2. Singh's father is a Professor at Yale university.

3. A typical pre-med program includes courses in Chemistry, Biology, and Calculus.

4. During the Winter, the hotel's revenues went down 30 percent.

5. When asked how he became a war hero, John F. Kennedy said, "it was absolutely involuntary. They sank my boat."

6. During the renaissance, many art forms saw a revival based on greek and roman influences.

7. Last Summer, we visited the grand canyon, Hoover dam, and the badlands of South Dakota.

8. The coronation of queen Elizabeth II was the first one broadcast over television.

9. The tropic of capricorn lies south of the equator; the tropic of cancer lies north.

10. Although web sites can be useful sources of information, much of what is published on the internet is of questionable value.

EXERCISE 21-3: Review

Correct the use of capitals in the paragraph below.

    Anyone who has wondered at the power it takes to sing the leads in operas such as Otello or Madame Butterfly will appreciate the fragility of the operatic voice. An article in the may 6, 1991 issue of *Time* Magazine, "Why golden voices fade," explores the choices opera Stars have to make in order to preserve their voices. A singer simply cannot sing demanding parts and expect his or her voice to remain pure. In fact, what is true of Opera Singers is also true of others who use their voices professionally. Lecturers and actors must also worry about what Doctors refer to as voice abuse, or the excessive and improper use of the vocal chords. A Senator who spends a great deal of time addressing large groups will fight laryngitis far more often than someone who doesn't speak publicly.

According to italian operatic legend Luciano Pavarotti, people who use their voices for a living—especially opera singers—must treat their Vocal Chords like precious jewels. One who does not care for his or her voice will have a short career.

CHAPTER 22

Using Italics

For use with Chapter 49 of *The Academic Writer's Handbook*

EXERCISE 22-1: Using italics

In the following sentences, underline words that should be italicized, and circle words that should not. Circle the number of any correct sentences.

EXAMPLE: In the months following the assassination, the country became *obsessed* with it.

1. *Idlewild Airport* in New York was renamed *Kennedy Airport*; schools were named after the dead President; even *children* were named after him.

2. Marguerite Oswald, mother of the alleged assassin, was interviewed on the CBS Evening News.

3. Jim Bishop's book, The Day Kennedy was Shot, became a national bestseller.

4. Stories with titles like *"Did Oswald Act Alone?"* appeared in newspapers.

5. Even in foreign newspapers like Paris's *Le Monde*, articles appeared for months after the assassination.
6. When writing about Oswald, reporters had to remember the meaning of the word alleged.
7. The CBS program 60 Minutes conducted its own critique of the *Warren Commission Report*.
8. As late as 1978, the *U.S. Congress* commissioned an investigation of the assassination.
9. Five years after the assassination, the country was abuzz with talk about the President's widow *marrying* Greek tycoon Aristotle Onassis.
10. In 1991, Oliver Stone completed a film called JFK, based on the conspiracy theories.

Using Italics 195

EXERCISE 22-2: Using italics

Underline any words needing italics in the following sentences.

EXAMPLE: In the Bible, Job says he is escaped with the skin of his teeth, not by it.

REVISION: In the Bible, Job says he is escaped <u>with</u> the skin of his teeth, not <u>by</u> it.

1. In 1986 the space shuttle challenger exploded shortly after liftoff, killing Christa Mcauliffe.

2. A lawyer who performs pro bono work does so for no fee.

3. Gavidae common, the latin name for the common loon, is also the name of a mall in minneapolis.

4. The word sparrowgrass is used in some regional dialects to refer to asparagus.

5. His reasoning was filled with one non sequitur after the other.

6. Director Woody Allen and actress Diane Keaton each won an Academy Award in 1977 for their work on the movie Annie Hall.

7. The motto of the District of Columbia is justitia omnibus, which means "justice for all."

EXERCISE 22-3: Using italics

Underline any words needing italics in the following sentences.

EXAMPLE: The ante in antebellum means "before," not "against."

REVISION: The *ante* in <u>antebellum</u> means "before," not "against."

1. The New York Times Web site is http://www.nytimes.com.

2. The moral of Hitchcock's Psycho may be simply that "Crime doesn't pay."

3. The superscript initials TM indicate a registered trademark.

4. A play that begins in media res begins in the middle of things.

5. It's easy to remember that stalactites hang down from the roof of a cave if you think of how the letter T looks.

6. My bête noire was calculus—until I found a good tutor.

7. The spelling rule of "i before e except after c" has a number of exceptions, such as foreign, leisure, protein, their, and weird.

8. Be sure to ask for Kurt Johnson, not Kirk Johnson.

9. The President's plane, Air Force One, landed this afternoon.

10. My favorite Mozart opera, The Magic Flute, contains some of the highest notes written for the soprano voice.

CHAPTER 23

Using Abbreviations

For use with Chapter 50 of *The Academic Writer's Handbook*

EXERCISE 23-1: Using abbreviations

In the following sentences, correct the use of abbreviations. Circle the number of any correct sentences.

EXAMPLE: The DEA (United States Drug Enforcement Agency) considers the city of Cali to be the center of drug activity in Colombia.

REVISION: The United States Drug Enforcement Agency (DEA) considers the city of Cali to be the center of drug activity in Colombia.

1. According to DEA officials, members of the Cali cartel have connections in NYC, L.A., and many other cities in N. America.

2. One DEA official called the leader of the Cali cartel "my Prof. Moriarty," referring to the archenemy of Mister S. Holmes.

3. The United States Justice Dept. has been trying to extradite members of the cartel for years.

4. The FBI uncovered a New York Department of Motor Vehicles operation in which cartel members were issued drivers' licenses and car registrations.

5. The Cali cartel is run like a major corp., complete with CPAs and other managers.

6. One would have trouble picking out a cartel operative on the st., even though the car he is driving might contain hundreds of kgs. of cocaine.

7. In Apr. 1988, U.S. Customers inspectors seized a freighter in Fla., and found cocaine hidden in wooden planks; but fewer than 10 percent of the planks had cocaine in them.

8. Care and ingenuity allow the cartel to bypass customs; e.g., they once transported cocaine in toxic chem. drums.

9. In addition to its U.S. operations, the cartel also ships cocaine to W. Europe and Japan.

10. The Cali cartel is worth billions of $; it will take millions to shut it down.

Using Abbreviations 199

EXERCISE 23-2: Using abbreviations correctly

Correct any errors in the use of abbreviations and numbers in the sentences below.

EXAMPLE: The company relocated its headquarters to MI.
REVISION: The company relocated its headquarters to Michigan.

1. Doctor Paula Tremont is in charge of the ER.
2. Aristotle wrote ca. 340 before Christ.
3. Ahmed is leaving in the p.m.
4. To remove an ink stain, soak the fabric in one to four tbsp. of ammonia in a qt. of water.
5. N.B.C. has the #1 morning show.
6. The seminar will be conducted by Lisa Sharp PhD at 3:00 pm.
7. Prescriptive rules of grammar (e.g. "Don't end a sentence with a preposition") are often based on Latin models.
8. That decision will be up to the president, ie, George Bush.
9. According to long-range forecasts, the weather in the N.E. should be unusually pleasant next summer.
10. School supplies such as pencils, papers, markers, etc are usually on sale in Aug. and Sept.

EXERCISE 23-3: Review

Correct the use of abbreviations in the following paragraph.

Washington, District of Columbia is the home of many important organizations. Most federal govt. organizations—the Treasury, the Mint, the F.B.I., etc.—have their headquarters in Washington. But there are also a number of private organizations, among them seventy think tanks, i.e., organizations devoted to studying issues in depth. On May 6, 1916, the oldest and most prestigious of Washington's think tanks was born. The Brookings Institute was known throughout much of the century as a liberal organization, but in the early 1970s it made a conscious effort to move toward a more central political position. Some people in the capital praise this move, while others, such as those at the EPI (Economic Policy Institute) feel that the liberal bent of Brookings balanced such conservative think tanks as The American Enterprise Institute and the Heritage Foundation. Brookings scholars spend their time thinking and writing books, most of which sell fewer than 5,000 copies. But their impact these days comes from television exposure. All of the major broadcast news organizations look to Brookings scholars for commentary. Of the seventy think tanks in Washington, only about fifteen are very well known or influential. Brookings is at the top of that list.

CHAPTER 24

Using Numbers

For use with Chapter 51 of *The Academic Writer's Handbook*

EXERCISE 24-1: Using numbers

In the following sentences, correct the use of numbers. Circle the number of any correct sentences.

EXAMPLE: 40% of lawns in this country are subject to chemical treatment.

REVISION 1: Forty percent of lawns in this country are subject to chemical treatment.

REVISION 2: Of the lawns in this country, 40% are subject to chemical treatment.

1. People spend 100's of dollars on their lawns, sometimes more than they spend on their children's schooling.

2. In the nineteen sixties, people didn't seem to be so obsessed with lawns.

3. Now private lawns receive up to 5 times as much pesticide per acre as do farms.

4. One May seventeenth, nineteen eighty-nine, a young mother in New Jersey began to feel dizzy and vomit within hours after the neighbors had sprayed their lawn.
5. Professional services aren't the only culprits; four times as many individuals buy their own pesticides than subscribe to lawn services.
6. American lawns take up twenty-five to 30 million acres; if all of that area is sprayed with pesticides, then a good deal of environmental damage is being done.
7. Over 6,000,000,000 dollars are spent every year on lawn care.
8. Some experts say that the chances of becoming ill from lawn care products are ten percent higher than those of becoming ill from toxic waste dumps.
9. Of all the pesticides used on lawns, the EPA has declared only 2 safe.
10. 29 of the 34 most popular chemicals are known to cause rashes.

EXERCISE 24-2: Using numbers correctly

Correct any errors in the use of numbers in the sentences below.

EXAMPLE: 6 students were injured in the soccer game on Tuesday.

REVISION: Six students were injured in the soccer game on Tuesday.

1. 66%, or 2/3, of the students opted for the take-home final, even though it was more difficult than the in-class exam.

2. The nineteen-sixties were known as a decade of civil disobedience.

3. The state government has a surplus of 31,000,000 dollars.

4. This project requires 12 8-foot pieces of lumber.

5. 13,814 copies of the book were sold last year.

6. Up to 4,000,000 children suffer from ADHD.

7. 827 students had their registration accidentally cancelled during the power surge.

8. When my grandmother reached eighty, her hearing began to fail.

9. While I knew what to call the 90s, I'm never sure what to call the 00s.

10. At this school, only one fourth of the student population lives in dorms.

CHAPTER 25

Using Hyphens

For use with Chapter 52 of *The Academic Writer's Handbook*

EXERCISE 25-1: Using hyphens to join compound words

In the following sentences use hyphens where necessary to form compound adjectives; to mark prefixes or suffixes; to note fractions, numbers less than one hundred, or words formed with figures; and to prevent misreading. Circle the number of any correct sentences.

EXAMPLE: In the early '60s, we witnessed the color television revolution.

REVISION: In the early '60s, we witnessed the color-television revolution.

1. The third and fourth grade classes visited the new aquarium.

2. The candidate described herself as a middle of the road conservative.

3. One sixth of the graduating class had GPAs of 3.0 or better.

4. We can hope for a better than average return from this stock.

5. To sign into this page, you need to enter a case sensitive password.

6. George's work related experience is not as extensive as Brian's.

7. Still, he appears to a be a well rounded candidate.

8. By the early '80s, the computer literate population had mushroomed.

9. I was feeling left out when Sean was invited to the wedding and I wasn't—and then I got a last minute invitation.

10. I'm buying two 12 month calendars so I can have one in the office and one in the living room.

EXERCISE 25-2: Using hyphens

Add or remove hyphens in the following sentences as needed.

EXAMPLE: He has a better than average chance of being drafted in the first round.

REVISION: He has a better-than-average chance of being drafted in the first round.

1. Many communities sponsor alcohol free activities on New Year's Eve and New Year's Day.

2. This college offers both two and four year degrees.

3. The newly-upholstered sofa didn't smell quite the same after the dog slept on it.
4. Five-hundred travelers were stranded in the airport last night.
5. Three fourths of the students had done their homework; however, one fourth hadn't.
6. The State Department has advised against travel in that country due to widespread anti American sentiments.
7. I'll need to resign the contract because we've made some changes in it.
8. I was faced with the next to impossible task of convincing the police-officer not to give me a parking ticket.
9. A two hundred year old statute forbids spitting on the streets.
10. Despite the widely-held belief that Rottweilers are dangerous, some are actually being trained as seeing eye dogs.

EXERCISE 25-3: Using hyphens

Add or remove hyphens in the following sentences as needed.

EXAMPLE: A 15 year old horse is middle aged in human-years.

REVISION: A 15-year-old horse is middle-aged in human years.

1. We will need to reenter the data because we lost the diskette.
2. The third-graders spent a lot of time at the shark exhibit.
3. The industry will lose nearly $7-billion-dollars to work related injuries this year.
4. The post election commentary was especially intense after the 2000 election.
5. Most word-processors can keep track of multiple revisions.
6. Use additional white-space to make your document easier to read.
7. The paste-command can be used for text or graphics.
8. This product should not be confused with similarly-designed products.
9. In a recent poll, 60-percent of the respondents admitted to cheating on their income tax returns.

10. Many Hollywood stars sign a pre-nuptial-agreement before entering into marriage.

EXERCISE 25-4: Using hyphens to divide words

Rewrite the following words, indicating with a hyphen where the words could be divided at the end of a line. For words that can be divided in more than one place, choose the most appropriate place. Write out in full words that should not be divided.

EXAMPLE:
interdenominational   inter-denominational

1. vice-chancellor   _____

2. intrastate   _____

3. fraught   _____

4. Postimpressionism   _____

5. haven't   _____

6. runner-up   _____

7. even   _____

8. commencement   _____

9. reiterate   _____

10. onstage   _____

CHAPTER 26

Making Spelling Decisions

For use with Chapter 53 of *The Academic Writer's Handbook*

EXERCISE 26-1: Distinguishing homonyms and words with more than one form

Within each set of parentheses are sets of homonyms or words with more than one form. Underline the correct word in each set.

EXAMPLE: We were (already/all ready) for (are/our) trip to the (capitol/capital) city.

REVISION: We were (already/<u>all ready</u>) for (are/<u>our</u>) trip to the (capitol/<u>capital</u>) city.

1. Our nosy neighbor was just (dieing/dying) to find out if we left on time, so we slipped out of the house (discretely/discreetly).

2. We let the car coast (passed/past) the neighbor's house before turning on the engine, and (then/than) we made a (rite/right) turn onto the main street.

3. We drove (strait/straight) (threw/through) to the city, (where/were) we finally stopped for directions to our hotel.

4. It seems we had remembered everything (accept/except) the directions, which didn't cause (to/too/two) much trouble.

5. We drove (in to/into) the city in bumper-to-bumper traffic; all we could (here/hear) were horns and squealing (breaks/brakes).

6. We stopped to ask a woman (who's/whose) hair was bright purple (weather/whether) we were headed in the (rite/right/write) direction.

7. I'd never (scene/seen) such a (cite/site/sight) before, and I could hardly keep my eyes (of/off) her.

8. "(Its/It's) just down (two/too/two) blocks, and (bare/bear) left at the (forth/fourth) donut shop."

9. The (affect/effect) that hair had on us was magical: we were (no/know) longer edgy or (board/bored).

10. We wondered (allowed/aloud) if we'd (meat/mete/meet) (anymore/any more) characters like this before our trip was over.

Making Spelling Decisions 215

EXERCISE 26-2: Distinguishing between homonyms

Choose five sets of words from the list of homonyms and near homonyms. If possible, choose sets that you have difficulty with. For each set, write one sentence incorporating all words in the set.

1.

2.

3.

4.

5.

EXERCISE 26-3: Applying the *ie* and *ei* rule

Using a dictionary if necessary to check your choices, fill in the blanks with *ie* or *ei*.

EXAMPLE
counterf_ei_t

1. sc____ntist   2. n____ce

3. sl____gh

4. l____sure

5. b____r

6. w____gh

7. exped____nt

8. d____ty

9. suffic____nt

10. inv____gh

EXERCISE 26-4: Adding suffixes

Using the rules from the text, combine the following words and suffixes. Use a dictionary if necessary to check your choices.

EXAMPLE
grieve + ance   grievance

1. place + ment   _____

2. mince + ing   _____

3. vacate + ion   _____

4. revile + ing   _____

5. fancy + ful   _____

6. city + fy   _____

7. dry + ing   _____

8. enjoy + ment   _____

9. artistic + (ly/ally) _____

10. excited + (ly/ally) _____

Making Spelling Decisions 217

11. slavish + (ly/ally) _____

12. pro + (cede/ceed/sede) _____

13. inter + (cede/ceed/sede) _____

14. irresist + (able/ible) _____

15. commend + (able/ible) _____

16. restrain + ing _____

17. quit + er _____

18. occur + ence _____

19. confer + ence _____

20. adroit + ness _____

EXERCISE 26-5: Forming plurals

Form the plurals of the following words, using the dictionary if necessary to check your choices.

EXAMPLE
wish   <u>wishes</u>

1. sewing machine _____

2. calf _____

3. church _____

4. carload _____

5. incubus   _____

6. editor in chief   _____

7. thesis   _____

8. analogy   _____

9. moose   _____

10. brief   _____

EXERCISE 26-6: Review

There are ten misspelled words in the following paragraph. Cross out the words and write them correctly.

One of the most important words to understand when talking about exercise is "moderation." The person who lifts wieghts seven days a week is not any healthyer than one who takes a half-hour brisk walk three times a week. What doctors have discovered in the passed decade is that moderate exercise can actually slow the ageing process. Exercise is advisible because it reduces the risk of heart disease, cancer, high blood pressure, and many other ailements. It may seem unbeleivable, but one affect of exercise is that an active eighty-year-old can be functionly the same age as a sedentary sixty-five-year-old. This is good news for men and women who feel guilty about not working out seven days a week. Now they can take their exercise in moderation and still reap the benifits.

EXERCISE 26-7: Revising

Begin your personal spelling list now. Go over papers that have been handed back to you recently and list all the words that were misspelled. Make two columns next to that list. In the first, write the words correctly, and in the second, write the reason for the misspelling. When you scan the reasons, you'll probably find out that your problem lies with one or two rules. Keep up the list, and you'll soon know which rules to memorize.

EXAMPLE
MISSPELLING:	CORRECT SPELLING:	REASON:
acceptible	acceptable	ible/able endings

MISSPELLING   **CORRECT SPELLING**   **REASON**

ANSWERS TO SELECTED EXERCISES

CHAPTER 1: *Constructing Sentences*

EXERCISE 1-2: Recognizing subjects and predicates
1. The Roman emperor <u>Titus</u> / ceremoniously <u>called</u> upon the Roman god of war, Mars, when he attacked Jerusalem in A.D. 70.
2. The prophet <u>Muhammad</u>, founder of Islam, / <u>attributed</u> his A.D. 630 conquest of Mecca to the power of Allah.
3. <u>Allah</u>, the one true god of Islam, / apparently <u>was</u> also <u>responsible</u> for the victory over Jerusalem in 1187.
4. The <u>sacking</u> of Constantinople during the Fourth Crusade in 1204 / <u>was undertaken</u> in the name of the Christian god.
5. The historical <u>term</u> "Crusades" / <u>refers</u> to the Christian invasions of the Holy Land, which was then under the control of Muslims.

EXERCISE 1-4: Understanding basic sentence patterns
                      v(l)   *sc*
1. Friedrich Kekule / was an architecture student. (5)
           v(t)   *do*   *oc*
2. Kekule / found chemistry preferable. (4)

EXERCISE 1-5: Using single-word modifiers
1. <u>Fans</u> <u>scream</u>.
2. <u>Promoters</u> <u>make</u> <u>money</u>.

EXERCISE 1-6: Recognizing phrases
1. infinitive/adjective
2. present participle/adjective
3. preposition/adverb

4. preposition/adverb
5. gerund/subject

EXERCISE 1-8: Modifying sentences with dependent clauses
1. Although other painters embraced abstractionism at some point in their careers, Reinhardt was an abstract painter from the beginning of his career.
2. When Picasso said, "My painting represents the victory of the forces of light and peace over the powers of darkness and evil," Reinhardt responded with, "My painting represents the victory of the forces of darkness and peace over the powers of light and evil."

EXERCISE 1-9: Identifying sentence structures
1. complex
2. compound-complex

CHAPTER 2: *Correcting Sentence Fragments*

EXERCISE 2-1: Identifying fragments
1. Fragment—no verb
2. Fragment—subordinate clause
3. Fragment—no verb
4. Fragment—no subject
5. Correct

EXERCISE 2-3: Identifying and correcting phrase fragments
1. Walter H. Annenberg is a great art collector, having spent a considerable fortune on works by the world's most renowned painters. *participial phrase*
2. The son of an immigrant who ended up in jail for tax evasion, Annenberg overcame many obstacles in his own rise to success. *appositive phrase*

3. Throughout his life, Annenberg has been known for his philanthropy, particularly making substantial donations to many art museums. *gerund phrase*
4. One of Annenberg's prize possessions is his Impressionist collection, one of the finest collections in the world. *appositive phrase*
5. This collection, as well as Annenberg's Post-Impressionist collection, will go to New York's Metropolitan Museum of Art after his death. *prepositional phrase*

EXERCISE 2-4: Identifying and correcting fragments caused by repeating and compound elements

1. The United States is one of a decreasing number of prominent nations to use capital punishment, otherwise known as the death penalty.
2. In extradition cases, the United States currently faces a problem—a serious problem.

CHAPTER 3: *Correcting Comma Splices and Fused Sentences*

EXERCISE 3-1: Identifying fused sentences and comma splices

1. One of the most basic items in the medicine chest isn't normally considered a medicine at all / it's usually found in the kitchen cabinets. *f*
2. Baking soda can be used a number of ways, / it can be a deodorant, a salve for mosquito bites or poison ivy, a toothpaste or mouthwash, or an antacid. *cs*
3. Tea can also be used to soothe bites or sunburn / it should not be used on a serious burn. *f*
4. Another kitchen staple that can do double duty is vinegar, / mixed with water it can be used to relieve "swimmer's ear." *cs*

5. Many of today's adults recall drinking ginger ale to soothe an upset stomach, / carbonated drinks of any kind still do the trick. *cs*

EXERCISE 3-2: Revising comma splices and fused sentences
1. One of the most basic items in the medicine chest isn't normally considered a medicine at all; in fact, it's usually found in the kitchen cabinets.
2. Baking soda can be used a number of ways: it can be a deodorant, a salve for mosquito bites or poison ivy, a toothpaste or mouthwash, or an antacid.
3. Tea can also be used to soothe bites or sunburn. However, it should not be used on a serious burn.
4. Another kitchen staple that can do double duty is vinegar: mixed with water it can be used to relieve "swimmer's ear."
5. Many of today's adults recall drinking ginger ale to soothe an upset stomach; carbonated drinks of any kind still do the trick.

EXERCISE 3-3: Revising comma splices and fused sentences
1. One of Wells's most famous novels was *The Time Machine*; it introduced Victorian society to the fascination of time travel.
   One of Wells' most famous novels was *The Time Machine*. It introduced Victorian society to the fascination of time travel.
2. When Einstein declared time to be the fourth dimension, suddenly physicists began to think of traveling in time as they thought of traveling through space.
   Einstein declared time to be the fourth dimension, and suddenly physicists began to think of traveling in time as they thought of traveling through space.
3. The laws of physics don't include anything to indicate that time travel is impossible; however, the possibility calls into question the foundations of physics.
   Although the laws of physics don't include anything to indicate that time travel is impossible, the possibility calls into question the foundations of physics.

4. On the one hand, time travel should be theoretically possible, while on the other, the implications of time travel upset the laws of physics.
    On the one hand, time travel should be theoretically possible; on the other, the implications of time travel upset the laws of physics.
5. In general terms, the implications involve laws of cause and effect: How can the effect come before the cause, which is what time travel would allow?
    In general terms, the implications involve laws of cause and effect; in other words, how can the effect come before the cause, which is what time travel would allow?

CHAPTER 4
Using Verbs

EXERCISE 4-2: Identifying main and auxiliary verbs

1. These plans <u>offer</u> *(main)* financial incentives to workers based on production.
2. Some workers—but by no means all—<u>are</u> *(main)* thrilled with the plans.

EXERCISE 4-4: Understanding tense
Present: write, smile, go
Present perfect: have written, have smiled, have gone
Present progressive: am writing, am smiling, am going
Present perfect progressive: have been writing, have been smiling, have been going

EXERCISE 4-5: Using appropriate tenses
1. For a year before the girls in Salem Village began accusing local people of witchcraft, disputes over land boundaries had plagued the town.

2. In 1691, the village had been without a minister for years, but when Samuel Parris arrived he proclaimed, "Before the year is out, I will have swept the devil from your midst!"

EXERCISE 4-6: Understanding tense sequences
1. When the space program was in its infancy, nobody believed that so many astronauts would lose their lives.
2. However, if you consider the number of tests and missions in which astronauts have participated over the years, you will realize that the number is actually quite small.
3. Of course, we all remember the Challenger disaster of 1986, when seven men and women were killed.
4. Before final plans were made to memorialize the fallen astronauts, NASA officials had considered the issue for over a year.
5. The Astronauts Memorial Space Mirror, a tribute to fallen astronauts, is located on 13.5 acres of land at the John F. Kennedy Space Center.

EXERCISE 4-8: Using the subjunctive mood
1. Many riders think, "If I were able to wear more comfortable clothing, I could ride better."
2. But the rules dictate that a rider appear in the arena wearing a jacket, breeches, and tall boots.

CHAPTER 5
Correcting Errors In Subject-Verb Agreement

EXERCISE 5-1: Subject-verb agreement
1. has
2. constitute
3. glorify
4. acts
5. is

Exercise 5-2: Subject-verb agreement
1. Politics, according to some pundits, makes strange bedfellows.
2. There are three good arguments for voting against the referendum.
3. Each of those books has been made into a movie.
4. Neither Jason nor Madison was at the rally.
5. The Senate is getting ready to recess.

Exercice 5-3: Subject-verb agreement
1. One of the students who works with the seniors is setting up a bingo game for Friday night.
2. Despite advances, there are still too many people living below the poverty level.
3. Neither the lawyer nor his client was able to convince the jury.
4. Either of those abstracting services is a good source for articles on psychology.
5. A herd of ponies was grazing on the lawn.

Exercise 5-4: Subject-verb agreement
1. Which criterion is the most important one for ranking the printers?
2. To go to the Olympics is the dream of many athletes.
3. Measles is usually a childhood disease.
4. One of the biggest investments made by most people is buying a home.
5. *The Red Shoes* is about a ballet dancer.

CHAPTER 6
Using Adjectives And Adverbs

EXERCISE 6-3: Distinguishing between adjectives and adverbs
1. previously
2. startling

EXERCISE 6-4: Using *good/well* and *bad/badly*
1. *well* (modifies *drives*)
2. *good* (modifies *driver*)

EXERCISE 6-5: Comparative and superlative forms
1. When George Balanchine, the director of the New York City Ballet, died in 1983, he was succeeded by one of the youngest directors ever to head a famous company.
2. The 4-H member's entry was the most perfect rose the judges had ever seen.
3. Chicken or fish is a good choice if you are looking for a healthier alternative to higher-calorie protein sources.
4. Pizza is good, but I like calzones better.
5. Some of the photographs in his collection are unique (*or*: extremely unusual).

CHAPTER 7
Correcting Misplaced And Dangling Modifiers

EXERCISE 7-1: Misplaced and squinting modifiers
1. Concentrating on producing the movie itself, producers of the past rarely concerned themselves with considerations such as an advertising budget.
2. Within the last two decades, producers who thoroughly understood the business approved budgets for marketing purposes.
3. Television, which dominates the leisure lives of many Americans, seems to be the reason for the increasing importance of marketing campaigns.
4. Correct.
5. Early movie advertising on television consisted of a voiceover, usually a deep male voice, and a shot of the movie's title.

Answers to Selected Exercises

EXERCISE 7-2: Limiting modifiers
1. Where you are in relation to your siblings can have an effect on just your personality.
2. Psychologists say that birth order is as important as parent-child bonding to almost all children.

EXERCISE 7-3: Repositioning modifiers
1. To the public that bought over twenty million copies of his books, Greene's writing was the work of a master storyteller.
2. According to literary and popular culture critics, most novelists write either "serious" literature or "escape" literature.
3. Much to the chagrin of narrow-minded literary scholars, Greene's writing included both types of literature.
4. Greene remarked on a number of occasions that the writer should not be ashamed of being popular among non-academics.
5. As a young child and even as a young man, Greene was occasionally suicidal.

EXERCISE 7-4: Repairing dangling modifiers
1. Searching for the perfect seafood dinner, people consider haddock a good choice.
2. There is good reason for the demand for haddock, with its mild flavor and smooth texture.

CHAPTER 8
Using Nouns And Pronouns

EXERCISE 8-1: Using pronoun forms
1. Friends and families of smokers asked <u>them</u> to quit.
2. Twenty years after the first announcement, smokers were told, "<u>Your</u> smoking also endangers everyone in your vicinity."
3. "It's horrible to realize that it was <u>I</u> who was responsible for the health problems of my children," reported one smoker.

4. As pressure to ban smoking in public places grew, some smokers fought back, protesting, "<u>We</u> smokers have rights too!"
5. In the new health-conscious climate, however, <u>theirs</u> was a cause that was decidedly unpopular.

EXERCISE 8-2: Recognizing pronoun forms

Many smokers discovered that quitting made <u>them</u>[o] irritable, causing problems at work and at home. <u>Their</u>[p] job performance suffered, and spouses and children found that a reformed smoker isn't always a joy to <u>her</u>[p] family. Said the son of one reformed smoker, "Sometimes <u>I</u>[s] want to give <u>her</u>[o] a cigarette just to have a little peace in the house!"

EXERCISE 8-3: Using appropriate forms of *who* and related pronouns

1. The Robert Frost poem opens with these words: "<u>Whose</u> woods these are I think I know."
2. Reading Frost's lines to the class, the professor asked if anyone could describe the person <u>who</u> was speaking in the poem.

CHAPTER 9
Correcting Errors in Pronoun-Antecedent Agreement and Reference

EXERCISE 9-1: Pronoun-antecedent agreement with collective nouns
1. plural—themselves
2. singular—its

EXERCISE 9-2: Using gender-appropriate pronouns
1. A receptionist is busy tending to the telephone, while a security guard walks the lobby beat.
2. Once in the heart of the building, the visitor sees a business executive making deals and a secretary typing letters.

EXERCISE 9-3: Correcting faulty pronoun reference
1. Sinclair wrote *The Jungle* to expose corruption in Chicago's meat packing industry, especially mistreatment of workers and unsanitary conditions. The book became very well known.
2. Sinclair was one of a group of writers active primarily in the cities of pre-World War I United States, writers who questioned the morality of the capitalist system.

EXERCISE 9-4: Correcting faulty pronoun reference
1. People's attitudes toward alcohol are ambivalent. People understand the dangers, but they live in a society that glorifies drinking.
2. Drinking moderately poses no health risks, but heavy drinking should be avoided.
3. Health officials are determined to educate people, and these efforts seem to be having some effect.
4. Even liquor companies, which depend on the use of alcohol for their profits, are beginning to preach moderation.
5. Not too long ago, some people praised alcohol because it was a remedy for many ills.

CHAPTER 10
Correcting Errors in Consistency

EXERCISE 10-1: Correcting shifts
1. If a university received funds, it must provide a clear accounting of how it spends those funds.
2. Universities are granted funds by government agencies for scientific research and development; when they apply, they estimate what their "indirect costs" will be.
3. What are indirect costs? They are any costs not directly related to the research itself; they include administration, maintenance, and libraries.
4. For example, if a university were to apply for a grant from the Defense Department, it would estimate not only the costs incurred by conducting the research, but general costs involved in operating the university as well.
5. Some people prefer to call indirect costs "overhead," while skeptical observers call them "padding."

EXERCISE 10-2: Correcting shifts
1. Tennis elbow is when the tendons of the arm are irritated or inflamed.
2. The town's recycling bins are not being emptied often enough, resulting in an unsightly gross mess.
3. Everyone who gives a presentation on Thursday will have it videotaped.
4. The President said he will not veto the bill.
5. If he were to win the election, it would change the dynamics of the state legislature.

EXERCISE 10-3: Correcting mixed constructions
1. When psychotherapy is a success, the patient trusts the analyst. Success in psychotherapy means that the patient trusts the analyst.

2. Undergoing analysis can help many troubled individuals overcome anxiety.
   By undergoing analysis, many troubled individuals can be helped to overcome anxiety.
3. The success of psychoanalytic theory is responsible for the popularity of psychotherapy in past years.
   Because of the success of psychoanalytic theory, psychotherapy has been popular in past years.
4. One reason for the recent decline in the popularity of psychotherapy is the rigidity of its rules.
   The popularity of psychotherapy has declined in recent years because of the rigidity of its rules.
5. Few patients can benefit from psychotherapy, and the process is a long one.
   The fact that few patients can benefit from psychotherapy—and that the process is a long one—accounts for its decline in popularity.
   success.

EXERCISE 10-4: Editing Elliptical Constructions

1. Audiences in the United States loved Bernstein better than they did other composers.
2. Many consider Bernstein to be the greatest American composer to date.
3. Bernstein's conducting style was flamboyant, and his scores were lively.
4. Traditional conducting was far more formal than that of Bernstein.
5. His devotion to and belief in children led him to conduct many "Young People's Concerts."

CHAPTER 11
Correcting Faulty Parallelism

EXERCISE 11-1: Eliminating faulty parallelism
1. The Transcendentalists supported both abolition and women's rights.
2. Among the most famous Transcendentalists were Bronson Alcott, whose daughter Louisa May became a famous novelist, and Ralph Waldo Emerson, who wrote great essays and delivered powerful lectures.
3. Transcendentalism did not offer any clear set of beliefs; rather, it suggested a way to view the world.
4. While traditional Christianity believed that divine intervention was necessary to improve human nature, Transcendentalists believed that humanity could be improved by relying on its own strength.
5. Transcendentalism was an offshoot of Unitarianism, which had rejected Calvinism and embraced liberal beliefs.

EXERCISE 11-2: Creating parallel structures
1. The price for a flight to Acapulco is much less than the price for one to Bermuda.
2. When you become familiar with a search engine, the more efficiently you can use it.
3. The library will neither reserve books nor check them out within five minutes of closing.
4. In preparing a family history, look both at family documents such as Bibles, letters, diaries, and at Internet sites on genealogy.
5. Scrub the area with peroxide, iodine, and alcohol, and then apply a compress and bandage.

EXERCISE 11-3: Creating parallel structures
1. Using the Format menu, you can change the font, change line or paragraph spacing, and add borders.

2. It's not safe for children to play in or around or stand on the recycling containers.
3. The new software will enable teachers to perform several tasks:
   - keep a running total of each student's test scores
   - average of each student's test scores
   - factor in attendance as part of the final grade
   - calculate each student's class standing throughout the semester
4. Many speakers are using presentation software because it makes their presentations more professional looking and also enables them to import spreadsheets and graphics from other programs.
5. A high-protein diet allows the dieter to eat unlimited amounts of meat, but very little in the way of vegetables or starches.

CHAPTER 12
Being Clear, Concise, and Direct

EXERCISE 12-1: Eliminating wordiness
1. Many babies who would have died within hours of birth ten years ago live healthy lives today.
2. Even before birth, babies can be treated for some conditions.
3. Doctors can perform surgery on fetuses as young as 24 weeks.
4. Premature babies frequently suffer from developmental problems.
5. Some babies need therapy to overcome disabilities.

EXERCISE 12-2: Eliminating wordiness
1. William Griffith Wilson and Robert Holbrook Smith supported each other's attempts to lead sober lives.
2. Their experience was so successful that they wrote *Alcoholics Anonymous* in 1939, marking the beginning of the organization.
3. Alcoholics Anonymous provides recovering alcoholics with the kind of support Wilson and Smith provided each other.

4. Correct.
5. AA stresses spiritual values, often mentioning God by name.

EXERCISE 12-3: Revising for clarity and conciseness
1. The lawyer told the reporters that the verdict can only be decided by the jury.
2. I was fascinated by parts of the registration process.
3. Frank Lloyd Wright's innovative approach to architecture combined technology and aesthetics.
4. When preparing a will, consulting a lawyer is wise, but not required.
5. When you apply for your visa, you will need to provide details about your travel plans, including details about your flight number and departure date.

EXERCISE 12-4: Revising for clarity and conciseness
1. When you are painting cabinets, it is a tedious process to remove all the hardware first, but you will be glad you did when you see the final results.
2. Right now, we have two alternatives: continue on our present course of action or diversify into a new market.
3. If I am unable to attend the meeting, I will send a proxy.
4. Because it was founded in Detroit, known as the "Motor Town," Berry Gordy, Jr., named his company Motown Records.
5. The term "lost generation" originated in a remark from Gertrude Stein to Ernest Hemingway.

CHAPTER 13
Building Emphasis with Coordination and Subordination

EXERCISE 13-1: Creating equal emphasis
1. Garnishment involves taking money owed to a person by one party to pay off that person's debt to a different party; for example, the IRS may take money from a person's paycheck to pay off a debt owed to the IRS.
2. A protagonist is the main character in a story; in contrast, an antagonist is an adversary.
3. A mild vitamin C deficiency may lead to joint tenderness and dental problems, and a severe one may result in anemia or scurvy.
4. Civilians salute the flag by removing their hats, standing at attention, and placing their right hands over their hearts; uniformed military personnel give a military salute.
5. Monosodium glutamate is a flavor enhancer; however, many people have an adverse reaction to it, such as headache.

EXERCISE 13-2: Achieving emphasis with dependent clauses
1. When work began to be concentrated in factories, the time people spent on the job became time spent away from the family.
2. Time spent on the job began to take precedence because the worker's wages kept the family fed and clothed.
3. A worker who spent more time at the factory was viewed as a dedicated family man.
4. Women did not work in the factories unless they were unmarried, or at least childless.
5. Managers, because they were responsible for production, measured a worker's worth by time spent on the job

EXERCISE 13-3: Revising for emphasis
1. Because his fame had spread before he was seven, he was invited to tour Europe in 1763.
2. Throughout his life, he composed in his head, while other composers agonized over the clavier.
3. By the time Mozart was fourteen, when he had been writing sonatas for seven years, he had played for the crowned heads of Europe and for the Pope. The Pope conferred on him the order of the Golden Spur, but Mozart did not think much of the award.
4. During his early years, Mozart performed in Germany, Austria, and Italy, where several heads of state commissioned sonatas and operas from him.
5. Mozart, as did many composers before him, wrote music for religious occasions.

EXERCISE 13-4: Combining sentences using subordination
1. The Walters Art Gallery, opened in 1931, was founded by a father and son.
2. Although a U.S. passport is not required for travel to most countries in North, South, and Central America, a passport provides the best evidence of citizenship.
3. Many experts advise buying an inexpensive home in an expensive neighborhood because its property value is likely to increase.
4. After a bill is introduced by a senator or representative, it goes to the appropriate Senate or House committee.
5. Rachel Carson's book *Silent Spring*, published in 1962, marks the beginning of the environmental movement.

EXERCISE 13-5: Changing the emphasis in a sentence
1. Tattooing is becoming increasingly popular, even though it is subject to very little regulation or quality control.
2. The philosophers called the cynics, founded by Diogenes, were so named because of their dog-like sneer.

3. The Islam religion, which forbids the consumption of pork and alcohol, has more than one billion followers.
4. Before Shakespeare wrote his best tragedies, he wrote his best comedies.
5. I overslept, which made me late for work.

CHAPTER 14
Choosing the Right Word

EXERCISE 14-1: Using a dictionary
A.
1. dis pas sion ate   adjective
2. so le cism   noun
3. per i pa tet ic   adjective
4. trem u lous   adjective
5. hor ta to ry   adjective

Exact definitions will depend on dictionaries used.

B.
1. noun (adjective), verb
2. noun (adjective), verb

C.
1. wharfs, wharves
2. moose

D.
1. swam, swum, swimming
2. dreamt/dreamed, dreamt/dreamed, dreaming

E.
1. more possible, most possible
2. more quickly, most quickly

F.
1. slang
2. colloquial (or regional)

EXERCISE 14-2: Using a dictionary

A.
1. Synonyms: bright, transparent, lucid, unclouded, glasslike.
   Antonyms: ambiguous, cloudy.
2. Synonyms: corroborate, establish, verify, substantiate, make certain.
   Antonyms: refute, deny.
3. Synonyms: distrust, hesitate, question, mistrust, suspect.
   Antonyms: believe, be certain.
4. Synonyms: oppressive, unmerciful, harsh, brutal, extreme.
   Antonyms: compassionate, easygoing.
5. Synonyms: educator, instructor, coach, mentor, tutor.
   Antonyms: pupil, student.

B.
1. əméenəb'l
2. fáwrmədəb'l or fərmíddəb'l or fàwrmíddəb'l
3. gö'tə
4. eéthə or íthər
5. leézhər or lézhər

C.
1. from Greek *acros* + *batos*, "high walker"
2. from binary digit
3. from Nicholas Chavin, a French soldier
4. from Arabic *shah mat*, "the king is dead"
5. from Latin *fractus*, past participle of "to break"

EXERCISE 14-3: Analyzing the connotations of words

1. religious group: *Congregation* suggests members who regularly gather at a specific church. *Sect* suggests a subgroup that has refined or broken with the tenets of the larger religious group. *Cult* suggests an extremist or secretive religious group.
2. old person: *Senior citizen* suggests a person over (about the age of) 60, but suggests nothing about their mental or physical capabilities. *Geriatric* suggests an even older person who has succumbed to medical problems typically associated with older age. *Elder* suggests an older person known for his or her wisdom and experience.
3. young child: *Tot* or *toddler* suggests a pre-school child. *Youngster* suggests any young child under about the age of 12. *Brat* suggests a annoying, misbehaving young child. *Imp* suggests a mischievous but, in the balance, charming young child.
4. communicate: *Announce* suggests making a widespread public communication. *Expound* suggests giving a lengthy explanation. *Comment* suggests offering a brief observation.

EXERCISE 14-4: Choosing words from the right register

1. inspect
2. annoyed
3. wonderful; a relief
4. question
5. understand; follow

EXERCISE 14-5: Choosing words from the right register

1. tedious
2. jeopardized; got his client into legal trouble
3. loves
4. amusing
5. disgusted, appalled

EXERCISE 14-6: Choosing specific words

1. restaurant, bistro, café, diner

2. film noir, comedy, romance, Western
3. bungalow, cottage, mansion, rancher
4. bracelet, tiara, necklace, earring
5. Gatorade, mineral water, Merlot

EXERCISE 14-7: Avoiding biased language
1. fire fighter
2. chair **or** chairperson
3. nurse

EXERCISE 14-8: Avoiding biased language
1. To be able to throw a "curve" ball is the ambition of every young baseball player, while the tendency to "hook" or "slice" is a mental hazard for practically all golf players. What causes baseballs and golf balls to curve? . . . To study this problem, imagine yourself as a baseball pitcher pitching the ball so that it spins counterclockwise when viewed from the top.
2. Scientists, confronted with an individual thing, or a material, or a process in which they were interested, looked at it, if they were Aristotelians, in terms derived from the metaphysics we have just sketched.

CHAPTER 15
Using End Punctuation

EXERCISE 15-1: Using the period
Note: *US* can be written either with or without periods.
1. The end of World War II brought many changes to the balance of power in the world.
2. Much of Eastern Europe came under Soviet control. (Tito, however, successfully retained Yugoslavia's sovereignty.)
3. The Allies formed the North Atlantic Treaty Organization to protect western Europe from aggression.
4. NATO became known as "the protector of European democracy."

Answers to Selected Exercises   243

5. France and England eventually gave up many of their colonies The battle over Algerian independence from France was finally settled by Gen. Charles De Gaulle.

EXERCISE 15-2: Using the question mark
1. Did you hear the judge ask, "Are you sure this is what happened?"
2. The defense attorney asked why the child had changed his testimony.
3. Were the prosecutors and the child's father "playing games"?
4. The defense called in an expert of questionable status to support the mother's testimony.
5. Could the child have been prompted? convinced that his story was true? perhaps even provided with the story?

EXERCISE 15-3: Using exclamation points
1. As I started to sit down, my husband shouted, "Wait! There's a cat on your chair!"
2. As we crossed the crowded street, another pedestrian suddenly yelled, "Look out!"

CHAPTER 16
Using Commas

EXERCISE 16-1: Using commas with introductory and concluding expressions
1. Before the boom, people used herbs and natural concoctions to treat injuries and illness.
2. For example, camphor was often used to ease headache pain.
3. Honey, not cough medicine, was used to relieve nagging coughs.
4. Correct.
5. In addition, they have been taking advantage of unfamiliar medical treatment especially acupuncture.

EXERCISE 16-2: Using a comma and a coordinating conjunction between independent clauses

1. One of the characteristics of the contemporary suburb is that residents have to drive everywhere, but a new generation of planners is changing all that.
2. Because most housing developments have been built to accommodate vehicular traffic, pedestrian needs are often unmet; and that emphasis on traffic has contributed to the isolation of the suburbs.

EXERCISE 16-3: Using commas between items in a series

1. One of the problems most difficult to solve is chronic, widespread homelessness.
2. Homelessness has grown in the past several decades as a result of high housing costs, severe drug problems(,) and release of patients from state institutions.
3. Homelessness has emerged as a severe, complex problem in American cities.
4. Many of the homeless simply need jobs, medical care(,) and housing.
5. No comma—items joined by coordinate conjunction.

EXERCISE 16-4: Comma use with essential and nonessential elements

1. Langston Hughes, whose poetry expresses the frustrations of racial injustice, is studied in literature programs across the country.
2. Zora Neale Hurston, a contemporary of Hughes's, provided inspiration for Alice Walker.
3. Within the past few years, African-American art, which had not received much attention previously, has been discovered by critics.
4. One of the more respected artists is Romare Bearden, a collagist.
5. Essential—no commas.

EXERCISE 16-5: Using commas according to convention and to clarify meaning

A. Quotations, direct address, and tag questions
1. "I'd say it was either Mohammed, Jesus, or Confucius, wouldn't you?"
2. "Couldn't it be," suggested the lecturer, "someone more contemporary?"

B. Balanced sentences, "more/less" constructions, and yes/no remarks
1. Half the audience believed that Marx was overrated; the other half, that he deserved his position in history.
2. "No, I wouldn't consider Marx one of the most influential people in history."

C. Names, titles, dates, numbers, addresses; clarifying meaning
1. The lecturer was Kristin M. McArthur, Ph.D.
2. She spoke before an audience of 1,340 people.

EXERCISE 16-6: Eliminating misuse of commas
1. The international community first became aware of the corruption in the Somoza regime after the 1972 earthquake; relief funds were diverted to the private use of Somoza and his cronies.
2. The assassination of newspaper editor Pedro Chamorro in 1978 provided added impetus to revolutionary forces.
3. The Somoza government left Nicaragua in economic and social ruin.
4. Correct.
5. Dissatisfaction began as the government had trouble keeping the promises it had made.

CHAPTER 17
Using Semicolons

EXERCISE 17-1: Using a semicolon to join independent clauses
1. Dorris had lived for a time on an Indian reservation; most of his early years were spent in Louisville, Kentucky.
2. As a single man, Dorris adopted three children; he provided them with a family atmosphere.
3. One of his children had trouble learning; consequently, Dorris took him to many doctors.
4. The doctors in New Hampshire could not diagnose his son's problem; however, the director of an Indian program on a South Dakota reservation recognized fetal alcohol syndrome.
5. Dorris's book about his son, *The Broken Cord*, sold over 75,000 copies; the story has touched people across the country.

EXERCISE 17-2: Using a semicolon to prevent misreading
1. The refuge is used by hikers, who find the beach trails peaceful; by sports enthusiasts, who consider the ocean and river fishing incomparable; and by sunbathers, who recognize the beach at the refuge as one of the finest in New England.
2. Closing the beach is clearly an unpopular decision, according to the manager of the refuge; and area residents who depend on the beach for recreational activities have reason to be angry.

EXERCISE 17-3: Correct use of semicolons
1. Linguists insist that no human language is "primitive," even if it does not exist in a written form.
2. Use one of the following graphics formats: JPEG, GIF, or Bitmap.
3. The participants at the conference included Meg Ashton, Director of Development; Ben Suarez, Director of Personnel; and Syd Coleman, Director of Community Relations.
4. The air temperature is 5° F; the wind chill is −20° F.

5. Many players try to cheat in Las Vegas; as a result, elaborate security measures are in place in the casinos.

EXERCISE 17-4: Correct use of semicolons
1. A recent study showed that British women who drank at least one cup of tea per day had denser bones than those who didn't.
2. Some Supreme Court justices, especially Antonin Scalia and Clarence Thomas, tend to vote more conservatively than others.
3. Until the success of the Harry Potter books, it was unusual for boys to be attracted to books by female authors.
4. In 1981, 11,500 air traffic controllers went on strike; they were fired by President Reagan.
5. Examples of herbal theme gardens include Shakespeare gardens, with bay, calendula, lemon balm, and rue; Biblical gardens, with costmary, hyssop, mandrake, saffron, and sesame; and bee gardens, with bee balm, comfrey, mint, and pennyroyal.

CHAPTER 18
Using Apostrophes

EXERCISE 18-1: Possessive forms
1. actress's
2. its
3. master of ceremonies'
4. Melissa and Jason's
5. The Blakes'

EXERCISE 18-2: Distinguishing between possessives and contractions, plural nouns, and singular verbs
1. Doctors
2. their

EXERCISE 18-3: Using apostrophes in contractions and plural forms
A.
1. could've
2. they'll
3. we're
4. you'd
5. haven't

B.
1. 7's
2. r's

EXERCISE 18-4: Reviewing use of apostrophes
1. It's never too late to improve your study habits.
2. Reagan's and Clinton's administrations both lasted eight years.
3. Men's clothing is located in the back of the store.
4. While HMOs are often criticized, our local one works quite well.
5. A cliché is an overused expression, like "You can't judge a book by its cover."

EXERCISE 18-5: Reviewing use of apostrophes
1. Paula's and Chris' GPAs are identical.
2. The Smiths are going to Florida on their vacation.
3. Many cereal manufacturers are expanding into snack foods.
4. That store is having its fifth "Going out of Business" sale.
5. The Wilsons' contributions to the arts have been honored with a commemorative plaque.

CHAPTER 19
Using Quotation Marks

EXERCISE 19-1: Quoting prose
1. Ty Kim Seng is a boy who was "forced to join one of the mobile work teams instituted by Pol Pot for the Khmer children's 'education and well-being,'" according to Rosenblatt.
2. In talking to children of war-torn countries, Rosenblatt discovers that he has being "defining vengeance conventionally"; one child he speaks to says, "To me, revenge means that I must make the most of my life" (471).

EXERCISE 19-3: Reviewing use of quotation marks
1. Some critics call *On Golden Pond* Henry Fonda's best movie.
2. The definition of "fair use" of copyrighted material varies according to the type of material.
3. "Man was born free," said Rousseau, "and everywhere he is in chains."
4. The researchers warned the company that they would not be responsible for any injuries caused by the experiment.
5. In what one observer called a "breathtaking" turn of events, the Supreme Court reversed the lower court's decision.

EXERCISE 19-4: Reviewing use of quotation marks
1. Mannitol is used as the "dust" on chewing gum.
2. The author's third chapter, "The Language of Poems," defines a number of common literary terms.
3. According to an article about a new treatment for warts, "76 percent of the patients were 'very happy' with the results."
4. The city council members called for "an end to partisan politics," but unfortunately their actions have not contributed to this goal.
5. With respect to wine, "room temperature" can be defined as 65° to 68° F.

CHAPTER 20

Using Other Marks

EXERCISE 20-1: Using the colon
1. Many refused to take seriously the specter of child-informants; in fact, they scoffed at the idea.
2. Some, however, related stories of radio commentators urging children to inform on parents and teachers quizzing students about their parents' politics.
3. Correct.
4. Some observers see a similar situation with today's children, except that today, children are criticizing their parents for ecological reasons.
5. One eight-year-old wrote a formal letter to her mother: "Dear Mom: Stop running the water when you brush your teeth. Love, Leanne."

EXERCISE 20-2: Using the dash
1. These children spent the World War II years in hiding—an experience that was sometimes as frightening as being in the concentration camps.
2. One survivor describes her situation—huddled in a basement with a dozen other frightened children—as one in which the fear of being caught plagued everyone constantly.

EXERCISE 20-3: Using parentheses
1. According to one critic, "Beethoven's Pastural [sic] Symphony is his greatest work."
2. The vocal ensemble specializes in music performed without accompaniment (also known as *a cappella* music [literally "in the church style"]).

Answers to Selected Exercises

EXERCISE 20-4: Using brackets, ellipses, and the slash
1. "Those who gave Taylor his nickname ["Old Rough and Ready"] would be amazed at his obscurity."
2. Taylor died after serving only a little more than _ of his term.

CHAPTER 21
Using Capitals

EXERCISE 21-1: Using capitals
1. Kennedy was the fourth president to be assassinated. (The other three were Lincoln, Garfield, and McKinley.)
2. When Kennedy announced plans to go to Dallas, Democrats were concerned about his reception in the South.
3. Governor Connally of Texas met the President's plane, and the governor assured Kennedy that Texans would welcome him.
4. The general population was indeed receptive, except for a man perched in a window of the Texas School Book Depository.
5. A former Marine with a Russian wife was arrested, spawning rumors of a Communist conspiracy.

EXERCISE 21-2: Using capitals
1. To get to Carnegie Hall, turn north at Central Park.
2. Singh's father is a professor at Yale University.
3. A typical pre-med program includes courses in chemistry, biology, and calculus.
4. During the winter, the hotel's revenues went down 30 percent.
5. When asked how he became a war hero, John F. Kennedy said, "It was absolutely involuntary. They sank my boat."

CHAPTER 22
Using Italics

EXERCISE 22-1: Using italics
1. Idlewild Airport in New York was renamed Kennedy Airport; schools were named after the dead President; even children were named after him.
2. Marguerite Oswald, mother of the alleged assassin, was interviewed on *The CBS Evening News*.
3. Jim Bishop's book, *The Day Kennedy was Shot*, became a national bestseller.
4. Stories with titles like "Did Oswald Act Alone?" appeared in newspapers.
5. Correct.

EXERCISE 22-2: Using italics
1. In 1986 the space shuttle *Challenger* exploded shortly after liftoff, killing Christa McAuliffe.
2. A lawyer who performs *pro bono* work does so for no fee.
3. *Gavidae common*, the Latin name for the common loon, is also the name of a mall in Minneapolis.

EXERCISE 22-3: Using italics
1. The *New York Times* Web site is http://www.nytimes.com.
2. The moral of Alfred Hitchcock's *Psycho* may be simply that "Crime doesn't pay."
3. The superscript initials *TM* indicate a registered trademark.
4. A play that begins *in media res* begins in the middle of things.
5. It's easy to remember that stalactites hang down from the roof of a cave if you think of how the letter *T* looks.

CHAPTER 23
Using Abbreviations

EXERCISE 23-1: Using abbreviations
1. According to DEA officials, members of the Cali cartel have connections in New York City, Los Angeles, and many other cities in North America.
2. One DEA official called the leader of the Cali cartel "my Professor Moriarty," referring to the archenemy of Mr. Sherlock Holmes.
3. The United States Justice Department has been trying to extradite members of the cartel for years.
4. Correct.
5. The Cali cartel is run like a major corporation, complete with Certified Public Accountants and other managers.

EXERCISE 23-2: Using abbreviations correctly
1. Dr. Paula Tremont is in charge of the ER.
2. Aristotle wrote ca. [**or** around] 340 BC.
3. Ahmed is leaving in the evening.
4. To remove an ink stain, soak the fabric in one to four tablespoons of ammonia in a quart of water.
5. NBC has the number one morning show.

CHAPTER 24
Using Numbers

EXERCISE 24-1: Using numbers
1. People spend hundreds of dollars on their lawns, sometimes more than they spend on their children's schooling.
2. In the 1960s, people didn't seem to be so obsessed with lawns.
3. Now private lawns receive up to five times as much pesticide per acre as do farms.

4. One May 17, 1989, a young mother in New Jersey began to feel dizzy and vomit within hours after the neighbors had sprayed their lawn.
5. Correct.

EXERCISE 24-2: Using numbers correctly
1. Sixty-six percent, or two-thirds, of the students opted for the take-home final, even though it was more difficult than the in-class exam.
2. The 1960s were known as a decade of civil disobedience.
3. The state government has a surplus of $31 million.
4. This project requires twelve 8-foot pieces of lumber.
5. Last year, 13,814 copies of the book were sold.

CHAPTER 25
Using Hyphens

EXERCISE 25-1: Using hyphens to join compound words
1. The third- and fourth-grade classes visited the new aquarium.
2. The candidate described herself as a middle-of-the-road conservative.
3. One-sixth of the graduating class had GPAs of 3.0 or better.
4. We can hope for a better-than-average return from this stock.
5. To sign into this page, you need to enter a case-sensitive password.

EXERCISE 25-2: Using hyphens
1. Many communities sponsor alcohol-free activities on New Year's Eve and New Year's Day.
2. This college offers both two- and four-year degrees.
3. The newly upholstered sofa didn't smell quite the same after the dog slept on it.
4. Five hundred travelers were stranded in the airport last night.
5. Three-fourths of the students had done their homework; however, one-fourth hadn't.

EXERCISE 25-3: Using hyphens
1. We will need to re-enter the data because we lost the diskette.
2. The third graders spent a lot of time at the shark exhibit.
3. The industry will lose nearly $7 billion to work-related injuries this year.
4. The post-election commentary was especially intense after the 2000 election.
5. Most word processors can keep track of multiple revisions.

EXERCISE 25-4: Using hyphens to divide words
1. vice-chancellor
2. intra-state
3. fraught
4. Post-impressionism
5. haven't

CHAPTER 26
Making Spelling Decisions

EXERCISE 26-1: Distinguishing homonyms and words with more than one form
1. dying, discreetly
2. past, then, right
3. straight, through, where
4. except, too
5. into, hear, brakes

EXERCISE 26-3: Applying the *ie* and *ei* rule
1. scientist
2. niece
3. sleigh
4. leisure
5. bier

EXERCISE 26-4: Adding suffixes
1. placement
2. mincing
3. vacation
4. reviling
5. fanciful

EXERCISE 26-5: Forming plurals
1. sewing machines
2. calves
3. churches
4. carloads
5. incubi (or incubuses)